MICROGREENS

MICROGREENS

The Insiders Secrets To Growing Gourmet Greens & Building A Wildly Successful Microgreen Business

CLIVE WOODS
Donny Greens

KLG Publishing

CONTENTS

Introduction	2
1 What Are Microgreens? And Why You Should Be Eating Them	7
2 The Equipment You'll Need	15
3 Various Growing Techniques & Lighting Optimization	19
4 Simple 6-Step Growing Instructions	32
5 Troubleshooting & FAQs	40
6 Simple Home Microgreen Recipes	50
7 Let's Get To Business	71

VI - CONTENTS

8
Market Research & Planning — 85

9
The Great Organic Debate — 96

10
Microgreen Economics 101 — 99

11
Testing, Sterilizing, Storing, Compositing & Labelling — 105

12
Creating The Perfect Harvesting Conditions — 115

13
Microgreen Marketing & Sales — 125

14
Guest Chapter with Donny Greens — 131

Conclusion — 145

References — 149

Acknowledgements — 156

Copyright © 2022 by Clive Woods

All rights reserved. No part of this book may be reproduced in any manner whatsoever without written permission except in the case of brief quotations embodied in critical articles and reviews.

First Printing, 2022

ISBN: 9781913666545

Contact: knglgn97@gmail.com

Books in this Series

Aquaponics: Raising Fish & Growing an Abundance of Tasty, Organic Vegetables – Without the Confusion & Cycling Problems!
   Written by Margaret Fisher, edited by Clive Woods

Microgreens: The Insiders' Secrets To Growing Gourmet Greens & Building A Wildly Successful Microgreen Business
   Written by Clive Woods and Donny Greens

Bonsai: The Art of Not Killing Your First Tree – A Guide for Beginners
   Written by Clive Woods

Introduction

If you've eaten at an upscale restaurant or trendy café in recent years, you've probably experienced the delight of eating microgreens. Likewise, you may have also seen microgreens for sale at your local farmer's market. But, when you went to buy some microgreens of your own, you were horrified at how expensive these tiny little plants can be. Now you're wondering, what are microgreens, and why are they in such high demand? How is it that people can grow miniature versions of well-known vegetables and sell them for such high prices?

You've maybe heard of people creating lucrative businesses growing and selling microgreens. You may have even heard that growing microgreens is a surprisingly simple business with high returns and low start-up costs. But how do you get started? How do you know if you can even grow microgreens in your part of the world, and where do you buy the special seeds and equipment you'll need? At first glance, creating a business growing and selling microgreens can seem like a daunting task. If that's where you're at, you've arrived at the right place. In this book, you will discover the exciting world of microgreens. We'll start by looking at microgreens themselves—what they are, why they are in such hot demand, and what are the benefits of adding microgreens to you and your family's everyday diet.

Next, we'll take a close look at growing microgreens. There, you'll soon discover that cultivating and harvesting microgreens can be just as fast and straightforward as you may have heard. We'll explore everything you need to know about the different techniques to grow microgreens, along with easy-to-follow and step-by-step instructions to take you from start to finish. By that point, you might have some burning questions on your mind. We'll then go through some of the most commonly asked questions about microgreens—everything you may be wondering about eating, growing, and selling these tiny plants. From there, we will detail some exciting recipes that prominently feature microgreens, so you can see for yourself just how versatile microgreens can be.

The following chapters will discuss the commercial aspects of starting and building your own microgreen business. You'll learn how to undertake market research, how to select your crops, and how to know if a microgreens growing business is the right choice for you. We'll take a look at finding your buyers and discover practical ways of marketing your microgreens, so you'll have plenty of demand for your product.

At this point, you might be wondering who I am and why I feel authorized to advise you on the nutritional benefits of microgreens and the profitability of a microgreens growing business. My name is Clive Woods, and I have been a professional gardener since I was a teenager. My parents were keen gardeners, and I spent most of my formative years outside in nature, soaking up all my parents' knowledge and enthusiasm about plants, flowers, fruits, and vegetables. It was inevitable that I would inherit my parents' love of nature and plants, and I soon went on to build a gardening lifestyle of my own.

Over the years, I have dabbled in almost every variety and method of gardening. But just five years ago, I discovered the world of microgreens, and that has since become my primary focus. When I first heard the claims that microgreens contain as much as 40 times the concentration of nutrients compared to their full-size plant counterparts, I was skeptical. But after growing and eating microgreens myself, I now know that there is undoubtedly some truth to this. I have learned so much about growing microgreens and have some close friends actively involved (and excelling) in selling microgreens for profit, one of whom will be introduced in a later chapter. The time has come for me to pass my knowledge on to you.

The benefits of growing microgreens are numerous. From a business perspective, a microgreen business is a low-cost, high-profit, and even an enjoyable endeavor (which is hard to say about most businesses!). Microgreens grow year-round and are one of the fastest crops to grow and cultivate, with most varieties ready to harvest and sell within ten days.

Microgreens also offer remarkable environmental, nutritional, and social benefits. By producing microgreens and selling them to your local community, you will be actively encouraging people to improve their health and the nutritional content of the food they serve their children. As an environmentally-friendly business, microgreens production is a sustainable and long-term business that you can run from your own home year-round. But don't just take my word for it, because in Chapter 14, I'll hand the reins over to Don DiLillo, the founder of Finest Foods NY & DonnyGreens.com. Don has created an incredible microgreen growing business, generating revenue of more than US $8,000 each and every month. Don will go into detail and discuss how and why he started, what he's up to now, and his top tips for starting a microgreen business. He'll also include his thoughts about what he sees for the future of microgreens from a business standpoint.

With the advice and knowledge gained from this book, you will be fully equipped to go from beginner to expert grower in the shortest period of time possible. After all, if a full crop of microgreens can be germinated, grown, harvested, and sold in less than ten days, why can't you take yourself from a complete newbie to a microgreens expert in the time it takes to read this book?

If you're ready to start learning about the exciting world of microgreens and how you can profit from running an enjoyable home-based business, read on! Microgreens are a hot topic right now, yet demand for these tiny nutrition-packed plants is consistently exceeding levels of supply. It's time for you to stay ahead of the pack and build your microgreens empire before everyone else catches on. The market is ready and waiting for you to learn about microgreens so that you can start growing and selling your own beautiful and healthy produce.

This book contains everything you need to know about every aspect of microgreens, from nutrition to growing techniques and creating a profitable microgreen business. This book has been written to be a complete resource. You will likely return to the knowledge contained within this book time and again in the future when new questions occur or when a tricky new situation presents itself. This book includes recipes, growing recommendations, germination times, troubleshooting, and so much more. You won't need to go out and buy another book, guaranteed! So with that, let's get started!

CHAPTER 1

What Are Microgreens? And Why You Should Be Eating Them

The simplest way to describe and understand microgreens is as miniature versions of full-sized flowers, plants, and vegetables. Microgreens are edible seedlings that are cultivated and allowed to grow until they have started to develop their first true leaves, at which point they are utilized in a variety of ways: as star ingredients in recipes, colorful garnishings on the side of dishes, or added to juices and smoothies.

In scientific terms, a plant is classified as a microgreen at the point when the embryonic leaves (also known as the cotyledon leaves) have fully developed and the first signs of the "true leaves" are emerging and visible. At this stage of development, microgreens tend to measure between two and three inches in length. But this is where the similarities between different microgreen varieties end, as microgreens exist within an enormous range of colors, flavors, textures, health benefits, and nutritional values.

It may seem that unique or different seeds would be needed to grow microgreens, but in reality, the seeds used to grow microgreens are the same as those that would be used to grow their full-size plant or vegetable counterparts. Just about any type of vegetable can be grown in the form of a microgreen. Some of the most commonly grown varieties of microgreen include basil, cilantro, broccoli, sunflower, kale, radish, and pea. Still, there are hundreds of different varieties—some of which you've probably never heard of! The vast majority are easy to grow and delicious to eat. In Chapter 12, you will find a detailed list and growing advice for some of the most popular microgreen varieties, but for now, just know that there are more varieties of microgreens than you will probably ever attempt or need to grow!

Another distinguishing characteristic of microgreens is their exceptionally fast lifecycle. Most microgreen varieties are able to progress through all of their stages of development—from germination to harvest—in less than ten days, with all microgreens ready to be harvested within 21 days.

Next, one of the biggest misconceptions about microgreens is that they are the same as sprouts. While both sprouts and microgreens are a form of young vegetable, that is where the similarities end.

Sprouts are seeds that have just begun to grow but which have not yet started to develop leaves. Microgreens have grown further than the sprout stage and boast fully developed embryonic leaves, as well as the first sign of the next set of leaves, which we call true leaves. It may help to remember that microgreens start as seeds and move through the sprout stage before becoming microgreens. Another difference between microgreens and sprouts is that sprouts are eaten whole, including the root system and the seed, whereas microgreens are harvested by cutting the plant stem from the root structure. The roots and remaining seeds of a microgreen are not suitable for consumption. Also, sprouts are grown using only water, while microgreens are typically grown using a growing medium like soil or coconut coir. That being said, microgreens may also be grown hydroponically. In Chapter 3, we will go into more detail about different techniques for growing microgreens, as well as the advantages and disadvantages of each method.

The second common misconception about microgreens among beginners, as alluded to earlier, is the idea that a particular type of seed might be required to grow these miniature plants and vegetables. As confirmed above, ordinary vegetable and plant seeds are used for growing microgreens; it's merely the growing technique and harvesting age that makes microgreens different from full-sized plants. That being said, seeds specifically sold for sprout and microgreen production typically return high germination rates and are vigorously tested for pathogens.

A further misconception about microgreens is that due to their tiny size (compared to full-sized vegetables), they must have very low nutrient content. Well, it turns out that the opposite is true. As will be discussed later in this book, microgreens are highly dense in nutrients. Studies have shown that microgreens can have as much as 40 times the nutritional content (in terms of vitamins and minerals) as their full-size vegetable equivalents.

Microgreens are also a highly sought-after ingredient in the culinary world. The bad news for chefs (but good news for those considering growing microgreens as a commercial enterprise) is that in many parts of the world, microgreens can be challenging to locate and expensive to buy. A recent surge in popularity and media coverage has led to increased demand for microgreens. High-end restaurants and cafés with access to a regular supply of microgreen produce are keen to advertise this fact in order to attract health-conscious and taste-savvy customers.

It can be said that microgreens sprang to popularity in 2006. Since then, their popularity has grown in leaps and bounds, particularly in line with the explosion of amateur chef television shows and other types of cooking and food-related programs around the world. More and more people are becoming interested in using fresh, natural, and locally grown ingredients, with recipes being adapted and new recipes created to feature microgreens as the center of the dish.

Far more than just a colorful garnish, microgreens are a way of adding a burst of nutrients and spike of flavor to a dish. The popularity of microgreens has been further enhanced by studies (see study here: https://www.ncbi.nlm.nih.gov/pubmed/22812633) that have proven the incredible nutrient, vitamin, and mineral content of these tiny plants. Some of the best health professionals and doctors suggest living foods such as sprouts, microgreens, and wheatgrass to be among some of the healthiest foods on the planet. With increasing demand and interest for healthful living and healthy eating being a major driving factor, microgreens definitely align with current health trends.

Microgreens have a very short shelf life and most varieties can only be kept fresh for up to a week after being harvested. They require careful storage and refrigeration to stay fresh for this time. This means that unlike other vegetables that can be frozen, preserved, and shipped for miles, high-quality microgreens must be grown locally and consumed as soon as possible post cultivation. This has created an *ideal business opportunity* for small growers who wish to produce microgreen crops and supply them locally to cafés, restaurants, residential customers, health food stores, and farmer's markets. Once consumers become accustomed to the world of microgreens, it's easy to get hooked. For example, once you create a delicious basil pesto using basil microgreens at home (see Chapter 6 for the full recipe), it can be hard to continue making the same recipe with store-bought basil paste. The taste is just not quite the same, nor the nutritional value.

As microgreens can be difficult to source, many growers choose to start growing their own microgreens to ensure they always have a fresh supply to source their favorite dishes. Growing microgreens is not difficult to master and setting up doesn't require a lot of space. If you're only growing one or two varieties, you can utilize a single tray on a windowsill or benchtop. Primarily, you need to ensure that there is a decent light source near your tray—but we will go into what you'll need in much greater detail later.

Given they don't take up much physical space, microgreens can be grown in any size home. Apartment dwellers without a balcony or backyard can still make this work and will have ongoing access to a fresh supply of fantastic and tasty microgreen crops. Similarly, microgreens can be grown anywhere in the world and during any season. Regardless of the temperature and climate outdoors, as long as you can maintain an appropriate indoor temperature and lighting pattern, your microgreen crops will continue to flourish year-round.

Most people who grow microgreens commercially start out with growing one or two crops for their own consumption, before later deciding that they want to turn their newfound passion into a bigger and more significant money-making operation. Many of these farmers started out because it's cheaper to grow these vegetables than to buy them in a store, or solely for the convenience of having fresh crops ready to harvest and eat on demand. Or because they simply weren't able to source the microgreen crops they wanted locally. Later, Don will talk about why he thinks it's best to start slow when launching a microgreens business rather than diving headfirst into bold action and ruining your reputation.

Why Add Microgreens to Your Diet

The more you come to learn about microgreens, the more you will realize how highly beneficial these small but mighty plants can be. The benefits of microgreens include the following:

High Nutritional Value

Studies have shown that microgreens varieties have as much as 40 times the nutritional content, including essential vitamins and minerals like lutein, beta-carotene, and vitamins C,

E, and K compared to their larger vegetable analogs. Broccoli microgreens, for example, offer forty times the nutrients compared to adult broccoli. The broccoli microgreen also contains sulforaphane, a powerful cancer-fighting phytochemical.

Unique & Intense Flavors

Microgreens come in a variety of flavors, from very sweet to very bitter, spicy, and even nutty in some cases. A small handful of microgreens can contain enough flavor to transform an otherwise bland and boring dish into a taste sensation. Speaking of sensation, some varieties like paracress will even leave your mouth buzzing, feeling like you licked a battery!

A Variety of Uses

Because microgreens are so often confused with sprouts, many people think they are nothing more than a colorful and attractive-looking garnish. On the contrary, microgreens boast intense flavors and high nutritional content, making them suitable for a variety of uses. Ideally suited for use in salads, soups, smoothies, and even dessert dishes, microgreens can easily be the focal point of a meal and need not be relegated to the status of a garnish. You'll find a multitude of unique recipes presented in Chapter 6.

A Rainbow of Colors

Microgreens are available in an enormous variety of colors, which not only serve to make microgreen recipes bright and vibrant but also represent the presence of a family of healthy compounds called phytochemicals, as well as other micronutrients. Health-conscious people know to include a variety of different naturally pigmented foods in their diet, as different natural food colors are beneficial for various areas of the human body. Have you ever wondered how fruits and vegetables get their natural colors? The color profile of a plant, fruit, or vegetable is attributed to natural chemicals known as phytonutrients. As a general guide, scientific research has repeatedly demonstrated the following to be true:

- Green foods are excellent for vitality and energy, help to detoxify the body, and boost immunity.
- Purple and blue foods can help fight inflammation, promote youthfulness, and protect against certain types of cancers.
- Red foods can improve the quality of the skin, reduce the risk of heart disease and diabetes, and help protect against certain types of cancers.
- White and brown foods are good for bone health, heart health, and can also protect against cancer.
- Yellow and orange foods can support healthy eyes, a healthy heart, and improve the body's immunity.

In the next chapter, we will take a closer look at the equipment you'll need to source before embarking on building your own microgreens empire. We'll look at the equipment necessary for people who wish to grow microgreens solely for personal use, as well as the additional equipment required if you choose to start growing microgreens commercially. Remember, you'll find all of the information you need about the commercial aspects of running a microgreens business in the second half of this book.

CHAPTER 2

The Equipment You'll Need

When growing microgreens at home for personal use, you will typically need all of the following equipment:

Growing trays: While any shallow tray will work, the most popular dimensions for microgreen trays are 10 inches by 20 inches by 1 inch. It is best to avoid trays that are deeper than one inch, as you will waste a fair amount of soil filling up the tray. Your trays will need to allow for drainage, and pre-designed microgreen trays will already include drainage holes. If you opt not to use a pre-designed tray, ensure you punch plenty of holes in the bottom to allow excess water to drain away. Most growers place a tray with holes inside a tray without holes.

Lights: Even if you intend on relying on natural sunlight to grow your microgreens, it's crucial to have at least one backup artificial light source. This ensures that your crops won't suffer from poor lighting during winter or on an unexpectedly overcast day. Lighting will be discussed in more detail later in this chapter and also in Chapter 3.

Nutrients: While a nutrient solution is optional, many growers (myself included) recommend adding hydroponic type nutrients to your water source regardless of whether you are growing your microgreens hydroponically or in soil. It will have a positive impact on your harvests.

The Scissor/Knife Debate: In my opinion, microgreens should be harvested using a sharp knife. The sharper, the better. Using scissors causes your crops to break down and rot faster, as the bottom of the stem gets pinched. More information on harvesting microgreens will be covered in Chapter 4.

Seeds: Seeds are arguably the most essential item on this list. It"s recommended that you source good-quality organic seeds from reputable suppliers. More information about choosing your suppliers is contained in Chapter 8 (Market Research & Planning For Your Microgreen Business).

Soil or Another Growing Medium: If you choose to use soil to grow your microgreens, a high-quality potting mix is all that is needed. If you're considering using another type of growing medium, refer to Chapter 3 for an in-depth discussion on the advantages and disadvantages of growing microgreens in soil compared to other mediums.

Storage Container: After harvesting your microgreens, they will need to be promptly stored in the refrigerator so that they stay fresh for at least the next few days. An airtight, food-grade storage container will help to house your microgreens following harvest.

Water Sprayer: You need to spray your microgreens with a very light mist of water regularly, and this can be achieved in several ways. If you're growing your microgreens outdoors, you can use a simple garden hose with a fine mist spray attachment. If growing indoors—as most people choose to do—you can simply use a spray bottle, watering can, or another portable sprayer.

Black permanent marker: This will be extremely useful when the time comes to label your boxes of microgreens.

When growing microgreens commercially, you will need everything listed above, as well as the following additional extras. Some of these items may seem like overkill, but it's crucial to take a professional approach, especially since your prized produce will be sold to and consumed by others who are relying on your farming methods for quality, taste, as well as health and safety. So here goes:

pH Meter: Plants are very sensitive to pH levels and when you're growing microgreens on a commercial scale, a pH meter will save you from a lot of guesswork. Some plants prefer an acidic environment, while others (especially Asian greens) thrive in a high alkaline environment. To increase acidity, lower the pH levels by adding a tiny amount of lemon juice to your water. To increase alkalinity, raise your pH levels by adding a small amount of baking powder to your water.

Plastic Packaging: Microgreens are typically placed in resealable plastic bags or small plastic containers or tubs with lids prior to sale. Often, tubs are the preferred option because they'll protect the delicate microgreens more effectively. The tubs will also need to be professionally and adequately labeled.

Weighing Scales: When growing microgreens commercially, you need to be able to weigh your produce to mark the quantity on your packaging accurately. Microgreens are typically sold by weight rather than by volume, and given that microgreens are an expensive product to purchase, your customers will want to know what they are receiving.

Soil Press/Tamping Tool: This is an optional piece of equipment that can save you some time when growing multiple microgreen crops at the same time. It is used for tamping down the soil to assist you when spreading seeds evenly across the soil.

Timer: Enables you to set your lights up to be on or off at specific times so that your microgreens receive the optimal duration of light each day without manual input.

Fan(s): This will allow you to ventilate your crops, which will help to prevent mold issues.

Warming/Heat Mat: Higher temperatures are undisputedly linked to improved and enhanced seed germination. Alternatively, if you happen to be growing microgreens for your own use and not for profit, you can just place your trays close to a radiator.

35% Food Grade Hydrogen Peroxide: This is useful for sterilizing trays and other growing equipment and proves useful as a reactive strategy in fighting mold. Some growers use this to sanitize seeds before or during germination, but often this is not effective and can lead to more trouble than it's worth. Some of the best growers out there do not sanitize their seeds, and instead, they rely on upholding a high-quality growing environment that doesn't lead to mold problems in the first place. We'll talk more about this in the pest and disease management section of the book.

CHAPTER 3

Various Growing Techniques & Lighting Optimization

At this stage, the thought of actually growing microgreens might have your mind wholly boggled with where to begin.

Maybe you've heard that many modern farming and gardening techniques utilize a hydroponic setup, where plants are grown in water—with no soil to be found. However, most microgreen growers actually prefer growing in soil over using water or other growing mediums. In this chapter, we will look at various growing techniques that can be used to grow microgreens and the advantages and disadvantages of each method. You'll also learn about the exciting subjects of pest control and disease management. In Chapter 2, we started to talk about the choice between artificial grow lights and sunlight. In this chapter, we'll dive deeper into lighting and discuss how to optimize your light sources to give your microgreen crops the best opportunity to thrive.

One of the most significant benefits of growing microgreens and one of the main reasons that many people choose to grow microgreens over other types of crops is that microgreens can be grown all year-round. When grown indoors, it is relatively simple to maintain a climate-controlled environment compared to crops grown outdoors. On top of this, microgreen crops are incredibly space-efficient and can take up as little space as a bench or a windowsill (if you plan to only grow a few crops at a time).

If you choose to grow microgreens commercially, you may like to dedicate a whole room/rented space for their growth and care. It is still infinitely easier to perfect the climate conditions within one room than for outdoor crops. Another related benefit is that microgreens can be grown anywhere in the world, including in countries with persistently cold climates, and even during winter.

Let's look at some of the advantages and disadvantages of growing your microgreens in soil.

The Advantages of Soil

· Many growers affirm that microgreens grown in soil have a consistently better taste than crops grown in other mediums. While taste is subjective, there does seem to be a prevailing view by soil adopters that the taste of microgreens grown in soil is superior to those grown hydroponically.

· It is much easier to grow microgreen crops in soil than to set up and maintain other growing systems.

· As covered in more detail in Chapter 8, a soil-based

microgreen growing system has a relatively low start-up financial investment compared to other options. The same cannot be said for hydroponic systems, which involve a significant initial outlay for the purchase of specialist hydroponic equipment.

· Using soil allows for easy growth and expansion of your business. Rather than having to purchase additional hydroponic equipment to grow a greater volume of crops, a soil-based microgreen growing setup can be expanded simply by buying more trays, soil, and seeds and allowing more space for the trays to be set up. When used in conjunction with a rack, trays can be stacked vertically to offer even more space and to allow for more plants to be grown simultaneously.

· In certain circumstances, microgreens grown in soil can be classified as organic produce. This will be explained further in Chapter 9.

· Soil that has been used to grow microgreens can be composted, creating a type of closed-loop where natural organic nutrients are recycled.

· Scientific studies confirm that soil-grown microgreens are more nutrient-dense than the same microgreen varieties when grown hydroponically.

· Some crops can only grow in soil. Beets and some flowers are prime examples.

The Disadvantages of Soil

· Microgreens grown in soil tend to be a bit dirtier and may need to be washed prior to consumption.

· Used soil will eventually need to be disposed of, which can be difficult for people who do not have access to a composting or soil recycling system. For example, apartment dwellers may find it difficult to dispose of used soil on a regular basis.

· Microgreens grown in soil can encounter problems with soilborne diseases, weeds, and pests.

· Growing in soil is seen as less tidy by some growers compared to when grown hydroponically.

Growing Microgreens Hydroponically

Growing microgreens hydroponically involves creating a nutrient-rich environment using water and fertilizer, along with growing pads or substrates. A variety of different growing pads can be used, including hemp mats, coconut coir, rockwool, and even clay pebbles. When considering a hydroponic microgreen growing system, you should consider the following advantages and disadvantages.

Advantages of Hydroponics

· If you already have access to a hydroponic type system, you can potentially set it up to grow microgreens without incurring significant financial expenses.

· The water used in a hydroponic system can be reused for multiple crops.

· Some crops consistently perform better in a hydroponic system.

· With no soil used in the growing process, there is no need to find ways of disposing of or composting your used soil.

· A hydroponic system is cleaner and involves less mess than a soil-based system.

· If you intend to take a live tray of a microgreen crop into a restaurant or kitchen as a sample of your produce, most chefs and business owners would prefer a tray of hydroponically grown microgreens rather than a tray grown with soil. Chefs obviously don't want soil in their kitchens because of sanitation concerns. It's also optimal to harvest soil-grown crops before taking them to show potential chef buyers.

Disadvantages of Hydroponics

· Setting up a hydroponic growing system involves a considerable upfront financial outlay to purchase specialist hydroponic equipment.

· Hydroponic systems can sometimes encounter problems with mold.

· Microgreens grown hydroponically cannot be classified as "organic" since additives and fertilizers are used in the water.

· Some crops have up to half as much yield when grown hydroponically, as opposed to when grown in soil.

· Hydroponically grown microgreens tend to have a shorter shelf life than those grown in soil.

Growing Techniques

So far, we have only touched on the generalizations of growing in soil versus hydroponically, but let's go into detail with some actual techniques available to you. The rest of this book will proceed on the basis that your microgreens will be grown in soil; however, it is also worthwhile being aware of other potential growing techniques that people have used to successfully grow microgreen crops.

A **wicking system** is a type of simple hydroponic system

that involves a rope or felt wick connecting a container filled with nutrient-dense water and another container containing the microgreens. It's a passive form of hydroponics, whereby the system doesn't have any moving parts such as motors or pumps.

An **ebb and flow system** (otherwise referred to as a **flood and drain system**) involves using a large container of nutrient-rich water located below the microgreen trays. It uses an inert growing medium rather than soil. A timer is set and attached to a pump, which floods the trays with the nutrient-rich water, often several times each day. Following each flood, the water is drained back into the container. This type of system can work well for microgreens; however, there is always a risk that the plants will dry out and stop growing if there is a failure with the pump or timer. Again, this is a hydroponic type system.

Deep water culture is another hydroponic set-up but of a larger scale and involves suspending microgreen crops in a special type of netting above a tray of nutrient-rich water so that the roots of the crops are suspended in the water, while the plants themselves do not touch the water. The water is oxygenated by way of an air pump. While this type of setup can be an effective way of growing microgreens, some say it is needlessly large and complicated compared to other methods. This type of system actually often works better when vegetables are grown to maturity, past the microgreen stage.

Aeroponics is a farming system that uses a series of fine mist nozzles with a nutrient-rich water solution. The plants are never submerged or flooded but are supplied with a fine mist. While some people have made an aeroponics system work for growing microgreens, there are others that argue that this is not an effective method for microgreens due to the plants' tiny root system. It's thought that roots as small as those found on microgreens may not be able to absorb sufficient nutrients and water from misting alone and thus need to be fully submerged instead.

Coconut coir is a type of growing pad that can be used with a hydroponic microgreen growing system. It can also be used as a soil substitute and is a popular choice since coconut coir is cheaper to purchase than a high-quality soil. It also has the unique ability to hold sufficient moisture while allowing excess moisture to drain away.

Burlap and hemp mats can also be used as a growing medium. Burlap is incredibly cheap to purchase but is notoriously difficult to use. When using burlap, it's imperative to control the humidity and temperature in the environment as much as possible—even more so than when using other growing systems. Many growers that choose to use burlap report it taking a lot of trial and error to learn the correct technique. Hemp mats, meanwhile, are an excellent way of transporting water evenly to all microgreen plants in the tray while maintaining a good air and water ratio. However, hemp mats can be quite flimsy and hard to handle, especially when wet.

As with any type of plant grown in soil, microgreens must be carefully managed to prevent damage from pests and diseases from developing. Damping off is another problem prevalent with microgreen crops, usually resulting from a lack of air circulation or, in some cases, due to the seed density being too high, or due to overwatering. Given the very short life cycle of microgreens—with the vast majority of crops going from germination to harvest in less than ten days—no pesticides are necessary during the growing process for microgreen crops. For this reason, it becomes vitally important that careful attention is paid to seed density, humidity, temperature, and air circulation. In Chapter 4, you will find a link to a calculator to determine the correct seed density for numerous types of microgreen crops. When used correctly, this calculator will assist you in warding off problems associated with high seed density.

While all microgreen varieties can potentially be susceptible to disease and pests, there are some crops that have an even higher susceptibility to disease than others. Mint, basil, and watercress, for example, are famously difficult to grow without encountering disease or pests at some stage. In particular, the presence of whiteflies and aphids is a common complaint among gardeners who attempt to grow these crops.

Another consideration is mold, which can occur due to the microclimate that microgreens produce when growing. Because there are so many plants growing close together, this makes them susceptible to diseases like mold and fungus. While mold exists in the air around us and we breathe it in constantly, it doesn't build up unless given the proper circumstances. The best way to prevent mold and other diseases is to have a clean, sanitary growing space, proper environmental controls, and use materials that aren't already problematic or contaminated. For instance, using home-composted soil from the backyard has a much higher potential for problems versus using a sanitary potting mix from a bag or bale.

Having procedures in place to ensure sanitation is also important such as disposing of spent growing medium right away, followed by sanitizing the trays. Over time, your growing skills will develop as well, and you won't make the mistake of overwatering, which can also lead to an environment prone to mold and disease. Be sure as well to have plenty of airflow and low humidity, as these environmental aspects are of utmost importance. If mold does happen to appear in one of your microgreen crops, you can use food-grade diluted hydrogen peroxide as a reactive measure. There are plenty of commercially prepared sterilization products, such as Zerotol 2.0. However, be careful because these products arrive in their concentrated form and must be carefully and properly diluted. These are harsh chemicals in their concentrated form and will thus cause chemical burns upon contact. Some growers choose to sanitize their seeds, but Don cites that these problems are more likely caused by poor growing procedures and contaminated grow spaces lacking proper environmental controls.

Regardless, every microgreen grower will experience pests or disease at one stage or another. You will inevitably come across these types of problems when growing crops of any kind, however by maintaining good standards of sanitation, careful growing procedures, and a well-controlled environment, you can go a long way towards staving off potential disease and pest problems.

Optimizing Your Lighting

Light is an absolutely essential resource for growing microgreens. Microgreens simply cannot grow without light, and an insufficient amount of light will cause microgreens to become pale and weak. Conversely, microgreen crops that receive too much sunlight can become 'burnt.' In this section, we look more closely at the different types of artificial and natural lighting options at your disposal.

Natural sunlight is always going to be the most cost-effective light option compared to any type of artificial light. However, natural sunlight is not always a viable option. For people who live in a cold climate or who are in the middle of winter, there simply may not be enough hours of natural sunlight each day to sustain a microgreen crop. Even in areas where the days are mostly bright and sunny, there will always be some level of variability. An unexpectedly overcast day can cause your current crops to suffer or slow down, making it a sensible idea to have backup artificial lighting available to use at all times.

Artificial Grow Lights vs. Sunlight

As with most varieties of plants, microgreens require a good-quality source of light to grow and thrive. When growing microgreens, one of the first decisions you'll need to make is whether to rely on natural sunlight as the primary light source for your microgreens or whether you will use artificial grow lights.

If you live in a cold climate or intend to grow microgreens during winter, there won't be much of a choice for you to make as you are unlikely to receive sufficient sunlight to power the growth of your microgreens. However, if you live in an environment that enjoys a good amount of sun year-round (or you only intend to grow during the summer months), it may be a viable option to rely solely on sunlight. Still, don't forget to have a backup artificial light just in case. For now, let's look at the advantages and disadvantages of sunlight versus artificial grow lights.

Advantages of Sunlight

· Sunlight is both free and natural. Using sunlight to grow microgreens won't increase your electricity bill, while using artificial grow lights will increase your monthly expenses.

· Microgreens only require between four and eight hours of direct sunlight per day, which may still be possible to achieve even during winter or in colder climates.

· Your ability to rely on natural sunlight will not be diminished if your windows have UV protection in the glass as microgreens don't require UV rays to thrive and grow.

Advantages of Artificial Grow Lights

· Artificial lights are an excellent choice for beginners, giving you a high level of control over the growing environment of your microgreen crops.

· Artificial lights can be easily paired with a timer, meaning you will know the specific duration of light exposure your crops receive and can then tweak that duration of light exposure until you find the sweet spot for each microgreen variety based on your results.

· Artificial lights allow you to grow your microgreens anywhere, even in a dark basement or attic, if you so choose.

Even if you intend to rely primarily on sunlight, it's still always a good idea to have an artificial light source as a backup. An unexpectedly overcast day, for example, could throw off the growth cycle of your microgreens. It isn't worth risking an entire crop because you chose to rely solely on sunlight.

Tungsten globes, halogen lamps, and incandescent light bulbs are commonly used sources of artificial light for microgreen gardeners. Incandescent light bulbs contain a thin wire filament that is heated by way of an electric current. Along with a wide spectrum of light, incandescent light bulbs also emit ultraviolet and infrared light. For this reason, incandescent light bulbs are not particularly energy-efficient as they are more focused on creating heat than light. While the initial financial outlay of purchasing incandescent light bulbs is undoubtedly cheaper than other options, you'll notice your energy bills soaring if you rely solely on incandescent light bulbs.

Compact Fluorescent Lights (CFLs) and fluorescent tubes produce ultraviolet shortwave light. As a popular choice among microgreen producers, fluorescent lights give off noticeably less heat than incandescent light bulbs and have a much greater lifespan as well as lower electricity usage.

Light-emitting diodes (LEDs) were invented in 1962. They produce low amounts of heat while being highly energy efficient. Despite their initial expense (compared to cheaper options like fluorescent light bulbs), LEDs usually turn out to be a more affordable option in the long run, especially in terms of energy usage. However, the main disadvantage of this technology is that LEDs produce narrower and shorter wavelengths of light, making them a less effective choice for growing microgreens, which tend to perform better with a broad light spectrum similar to that produced by natural sunlight. Furthermore, it's important to keep in mind that LEDs are highly heat-sensitive, so it's important to ensure that your microgreen growing area doesn't become too hot; otherwise, your produce may suffer.

A scientific study of kale microgreens showed that fluorescent/incandescent light promoted faster plant growth, but the LED lights produced kale microgreens with a higher pigment concentration, which may indicate a healthier plant was grown with LED lights.

From my personal growing experience, I tend to rely on sunlight due to living in a stable climate and a relatively bright region. So, when it comes to artificial light, what would I recommend? As it's difficult for me to give you the best answer here, I asked Don DiLillo from FinestFoodsNY.com. According to Don, the best artificial lights you can go for (especially when running this as a business) are called T5 Full Spectrum Fluorescent Lights. He says they are simply the best quality out there and that all the best microgreen business owners use them. He advises against using cheap LEDs shipped from China. If you're just growing as a hobby, it might be okay to just rely on sunlight, like me, or to go for a cheaper artificial lighting option. It's really up to you!

CHAPTER 4

Simple 6-Step Growing Instructions

In the last chapter, we covered the advantages and disadvantages of growing microgreens in soil versus growing via other techniques. Based on that information, you now need to decide whether to use soil as your growing medium or to use a hydroponic growing system. Alternatively, maybe you've decided that one of the other less common techniques would be more suitable for your situation and experience level.

Since most microgreen gardeners choose to grow their crops in soil, the following steps have been written with soil growing in mind, and you would need to adapt the steps below when using one of the other techniques. Having said that, there are many similarities across each method, so you can still learn from the method below, even when you're not growing your microgreens in soil. Let's get started with the most obvious place to start and that's Step 1.

Step 1: Soaking Your Seeds

The first step for growing microgreens is to pre-soak your seeds. It is important to note, however, that not all microgreen seeds require pre-soaking. In Chapter 12, you can find a complete list of microgreen seeds and detailed instructions on which seeds require pre-soaking and for how long. Make sure you check this list before growing any new type of microgreen as soaking the wrong type of seed may cause it to drown and fail to germinate or will lead to problems when the time comes time to spread the seeds on your soil. If your seeds do require pre-soaking, the process is very simple. Measure out the volume of seeds that you intend to use (the calculator linked later will be useful to ascertain the volume required). There is no need to rinse your seeds.

Put the seeds in a bowl and fill the bowl with enough water, so that the height of the water is about double the height of the seeds. Certain seeds absorb more water than others, so it can be helpful to note seed types that absorb more water during soaking. Wheatgrass seeds, for example, are notorious for absorbing excess water during the pre-soaking stage. Cover the bowl and leave your seeds to soak overnight for a maximum of 12 hours, unless otherwise specified in the table featured in Chapter 12. Over-soaked seeds generally have lower germination rates. For best results, soak your seeds in cold water. If you live in a particularly hot or non-airconditioned environment, it may be beneficial to place the bowl in the refrigerator during the soaking period.

You may find that some of the seeds will float to the top of the water during the soaking process. These seeds should

NOT be used. Floating seeds indicate a lack of viable embryos or a lack of nutrient stores inside of the seed. That being said, some seeds like sunflower seeds will always float. It is important to keep these kinds of seeds underwater during the soaking process by using a weight.

Step 2: Germinating & Growing

Following pre-soaking, run your soaked seeds through a strainer or colander again to drain off the excess water. You should aim to plant your seeds immediately or after no more than a few hours of letting them dry off. Make sure you're using high-quality potting soil. Level the soil out across the tray with your hand while not applying too much force or compressing the soil too much. Next, use another tray or your tamping tool to press the soil down, creating a flat and even surface to spread your seeds across.

With the surface of the soil even and smooth, broadcast your freshly sprouted seeds as evenly as possible over the soil surface. It is best for there to only be a single layer of seeds, as multiple layers of seed can result in mold growth. For some varieties, it's better to add another light layer of soil across the top of the seeds to help improve germination and the shedding of seed hulls. At this point, the seeds can be pressed again (using a tamping tool or flat tray) so that they make good contact with the soil. Once your seeds are in a good position, use a spray bottle or mist setting on a hose nozzle to slowly moisten the seeds and the soil.

During this first stage, your newly germinating seeds don't require light. It's a good idea, though, to keep them away from a direct light source, or, if this isn't possible, cover them temporarily so they aren't exposed to too much light at this stage of their development.

When your seedlings have grown a little bit further (have rooted themselves and sprouted up out of the soil), they will require daily sunlight. They will then transition from pale sprouts into healthy, darker-colored plants and will require full access to sunlight or artificial light for a minimum of four hours per day. To work out the correct seed density to use for your microgreens, we highly recommend this calculator: https://www.microveggy.com/selling-microgreens/ (scroll to roughly halfway down the webpage to get access to it)

Step 3: Light Exposure

Once your microgreens have properly sprouted, they will require between four and eight hours of quality light each day. This light can come from artificial sources as mentioned earlier or from natural sunlight. Regardless of your choice, the quality, exposure time, and strength of light your microgreen plants receive will have a direct effect on their vitamin and mineral content as well as the richness of their taste.

Take a fully grown, normal-sized head of lettuce as an example. If you cut a head of lettuce in half, you will notice a stark color difference between the darker, chlorophyll-rich green outer leaves and the pale and almost white inner leaves. You'll also notice a difference in flavor, with the outer leaves having a much stronger taste than the inner leaves, which can be almost tasteless towards the core. The same holds true for nutrients as well as taste—with the dark, outer leaves being much more nutrient-dense than the pale inner leaves. The differences seen in a single head of lettuce are entirely due to the effect of light, with the outer leaves receiving more direct exposure to light, while the inner leaves are not exposed to light at all.

That being said, different types of microgreens have different light requirements. If you rely on natural sunlight, it's a good idea to change the types of microgreen that you grow during winter to those that do not have as higher light requirements as others. Good microgreens to grow during the darker winter months include arugula, mustard greens, dill, cilantro, and many of the lettuce varieties. Remember, lettuce can come in microgreen form as well, which looks just like how you would imagine it to look like.

In summer, when natural sunlight is abundant, you can begin again to grow other microgreen varieties that thrive when there is greater light exposure. However, if you're using artificial lighting, you'll be able to grow all types of microgreen varieties year-round by manually adjusting the amount of light each tray receives with help from an electric timer.

Step 4: Harvesting

Before learning about microgreens, you probably never imagined harvesting a plant with a sharp knife but that is exactly the recommended method for harvesting microgreens. Microgreens are harvested by cutting the shoot just above the soil line. Unlike sprouts, microgreens are never harvested by pulling them straight out of the soil.

This is because microgreen roots are not suitable for

consumption and it is only the visible plant and stem that is consumed. You may be tempted to pull the microgreens directly from the soil and then cut the roots off afterward, however, this is not advised as the process of pulling the microgreens out can cause damage and bruising to the plants. This would also be a very messy process. Microgreens will need to be refrigerated immediately after being harvested. Most growers choose to harvest directly into the final packaging before refrigeration, without rinsing—as rinsing the plants would drastically decrease their shelf life.

Step 5: Washing

Microgreens are already a very clean plant to grow, especially since they are typically grown indoors and harvested above the soil or growing medium. However, it's always possible for soil, roots, seed husks, and un-germinated seeds to be found amongst the harvested microgreens. As a rule, make sure your product looks relatively clean when packaged. Customers typically don't want to buy a dirty product or spend time washing it. The most important thing to realize as a commercial grower is that washing your microgreens and offering them as a ready-to-eat product will change the way you are regulated. Ready-to-eat products are taxable and fall under the jurisdiction of the department of health. In contrast, raw agricultural products are non-taxable and fall under the jurisdiction of the department of agriculture.

Don recommends selling microgreens as a raw agricultural product (non-washed) since there is no tax burden and less labor, meaning more profits and simpler procedures. When a customer asks Don if they need to wash the product, he replies, "I'm legally obligated to tell you to wash these microgreens because they are considered a raw agricultural product, just like a tomato or a cucumber. This being said, I never wash them before eating them, and neither do most of my customers." This covers him legally while also implying that they are inherently clean and can be eaten without washing.

From a quality standpoint, microgreens will inevitably hold moisture after being rinsed, and this excess moisture—particularly in the cool environment of your refrigerator—can sometimes cause the microgreens to deteriorate faster than one might like. Nevertheless, the washing process typically involves rinsing with fresh water and then gently patting the microgreens dry with a soft cloth or paper towel (which can lead to bruising, plant damage, and faster degradation). A salad spinner can also be used to gently remove excess water before manually patting to remove any remaining water.

Step 6: Storage

Like all fruits and vegetables, microgreens must be stored properly to maintain their freshness and flavor. Microgreens can stay fresh for up to a week following harvest, provided they are stored correctly. There are two crucial conditions for storing microgreens: keep them cool and keep them out of direct sunlight. Of course, the best place in your home that already fulfills these two conditions is your refrigerator. A temperature of about 36°F (2°C) will keep your microgreens fresh.

Check the temperature of your refrigerator before storing

microgreens as some refrigerators are set to a higher temperature when storing everyday household items. If it's possible to manually change the temperature of your fridge, turning it down to the recommended 36°F (2°C) will give your microgreens a couple of days of extra freshness. Similarly, it's important to keep your freshly harvested microgreens out of direct sunlight. As much as they need sunlight while growing, sunlight exposure following harvesting can negatively impact the appearance and taste of your microgreens!

CHAPTER 5

Troubleshooting & FAQs

1) Eating Microgreens FAQs

What are the most popular microgreens?

The most popular varieties are pea, sunflower, radish, and broccoli.

What is the difference between sprouts and microgreens?

While microgreens and sprouts are often confused, they are two distinct types of plants. Most notably, sprouts are grown in water and are eaten whole, including the stem, root, and seed. Microgreens are usually grown in soil (although they can equally be grown in water) and are harvested by cutting, with only the above-soil part of the plant fit for consumption.

This question has been answered in more detail in Chapter 1 of this book.

How long do microgreens stay edible?

If refrigerated at the correct temperature, most microgreens will stay fresh and edible for between five and seven days. Some microgreens, like pea and sunflower, will last for multiple weeks. Microgreens grown in natural sunlight tend to have a slightly longer shelf life than those grown using artificial lights.

What is the nutritional value of microgreens?

Some microgreens, including radish, broccoli, and red cabbage, have been shown to have as much as 40 times the nutrients of their full-grown counterparts. Testing undertaken at the University of Maryland found consistently high levels of beta-carotene, lutein, vitamin K, vitamin E, and vitamin C in 25 different microgreen varieties. You can find the link to the study in the references section at the end of this book.

Do microgreens need to be washed prior to consumption?

Like all fresh raw foods, it is recommended that they are properly washed before being eaten. This being said, microgreens are inherently clean because they are cut above the soil. If you are the type of person who would eat a tomato right from the vine, then you would most likely do the same with microgreens. For commercial purposes, washing produce and selling it as ready-to-eat will change the way you are looked at from a regulatory standpoint. Ready-to-eat products are taxable and fall under the jurisdiction of the department of health, whereas raw agricultural products are non-taxable and fall under the jurisdiction of the department of agriculture. In the U.S, Don recommends selling as a raw agricultural product (non-washed).

If I'm allergic to a certain vegetable, can I eat the microgreens version of it?

Microgreens are miniature versions of full-grown plants with many of the same properties. If you are allergic to a certain vegetable, you should assume that you are also allergic to its microgreen version. For example, many people are allergic to soybeans, so these people should also avoid eating soybean microgreens.

If I'm gluten intolerant, can I still eat microgreens?

It's good news for people with gluten intolerance, as many plants that normally contain gluten in their seed, such as wheat and barley, are gluten-free at the microgreen stage. This is because gluten is contained in the seed; microgreens are the plants, so they don't contain gluten. It is only in the seeds of these plants that gluten is present. Of course, ensure this to be true for any crops you eat/grow before deciding to eat them. This book is not responsible for any actions you take as a result of the information provided (please refer to the disclaimer at the start of the book).

What if I'm taking blood-thinning medication?

You may have heard that people taking blood-thinning medication should be cautious about consuming large quantities of microgreens. This is because many microgreens contain high levels of vitamin K, the vitamin that aids in blood clotting. If you take blood-thinning medication, talk to your doctor about acceptable limits of vitamin K in your diet.

2) Growing Microgreens FAQs

Where do I buy the seeds required to grow microgreens?

People are often surprised to find out that the seeds used to grow microgreens are the same seeds that would otherwise be used to grow full-size plants. However, you'll need to purchase a lot more seeds to grow microgreens than their full-size counterparts, as the seeds are planted at a far higher density. This is why we recommend choosing a seed wholesaler rather than a retailer in order to keep your costs down. Furthermore, seeds rated for microgreen and sprout production typically have high germination rates and are triple-tested for pathogens.

What kind of soil should I use to grow my microgreens?

While some people choose to grow their microgreens hydroponically, the majority still prefer to grow in soil. Any high-quality potting soil will be suitable. Some growers choose to use soil that has been fortified with kelp or other plants, which provide added nutrients like Zinc, Iodine, Vitamin A, and more.

How can I tell if I can grow microgreens in my climate?

Regardless of the climate outdoors, microgreens can be

successfully grown in almost any part of the world. Most microgreens are grown indoors, where it is much easier to control the climate and temperature of the environment.

When do I harvest my microgreens?

In Chapter 12, you'll find a comprehensive list of microgreens and their average harvest time. As a general guide, you will know your microgreens are ready to be harvested when they have produced their second set of leaves, known as true leaves.

Can I regrow another set of microgreens after the first harvest?

Most microgreens varieties will not grow back once harvested, but certain types like pea and wheatgrass will regrow. Provided you harvest your microgreens properly by cutting the shoots off with a sharp knife just above the soil level, these specific microgreen varieties will regrow a new set of shoots. You'll notice that your microgreens will become weaker after several harvests, at which time you can empty the full contents of your tray and start again with a fresh crop.

How can I tell if I have mold on my microgreens?

Sometimes what can look like mold is actually the cilia or root hairs (part of the natural root structure of young plants). Here are some simple ways of telling the difference between mold and cilia: mold has a spider web appearance, is slimy, has a musty smell, and cannot be rinsed off the plant. Cilia, on the other hand, is centralized around the main root, has more of a hairy appearance, is not slimy, is odorless, and will temporarily disappear following a rinse with water.

If I do have mold on my microgreens, what can I do?

The most common way of removing mold from microgreen plants is to spray 3% food-grade hydrogen peroxide or white vinegar over the microgreen plants. Alternatively, use both substances and create a mixture of one-part white vinegar to one-part hydrogen peroxide. Always use this mixture minimally as too much can burn your plants. The best way to deal with mold is by taking preventative action (proper growing procedures and environmental conditions) so that the mold never appears in the first place. Prevention is better than cure, as they say.

Why are my seeds failing to germinate?

When seeds fail to germinate, it usually comes down to one of three possible reasons. First, and most commonly, the soil is not moist enough to support seed germination. Secondly, you may not have created the correct ambient temperature to aid your seeds' germination. Thirdly, low-quality seeds or seeds that have been incorrectly stored have lower germination rates.

My microgreens aren't germinating properly. What can I do?

Your first step should be to consult the extensive table in Chapter 12 to ensure that you are following the guidelines about pre-soaking. Some microgreens, including broccoli, for example, can drown and fail to germinate if the seeds are kept wet for too long. On the other hand, a common reason for seeds failing to germinate is a lack of moisture at the germination stage. Seeds and soil should never be allowed to fully dry out at the crucial stage of germination.

Why is my tray of microgreens germinating unevenly?

First, ensure that your entire tray is receiving the same conditions, including air circulation, light, and water. Is one part of the tray in direct sunlight while the other is shaded? Next, ensure that the same quality of soil has been used throughout the tray and that it has been mixed properly and consistently. This being said, the most common cause of an uneven microgreen canopy is uneven watering.

Why are my microgreens excessively tall?

It may seem counterintuitive but excessively tall microgreens often indicate that they are suffering from a lack of light. Rather than concentrating all of their force on developing a high nutrient density, microgreens that are not receiving sufficient light will apply all of their energy towards finding an improved light source. This is often referred to as plants getting "leggy". The solution here is to try increasing the quality and quantity of light that your microgreens are receiving. This may be as simple as moving your artificial lights closer to the trays. Alternatively, if relying on intermittent indirect sunlight, you may need to supplement with artificial grow lights.

How do I regulate the pH levels of my plants?

Microgreens can be sensitive to pH levels, with some plants preferring an acidic environment while others (especially Asian greens) thrive in a high alkaline environment. To increase acidity, lower the pH levels by adding a tiny amount of lemon juice to your water. To increase alkalinity, raise your pH levels by adding a tiny amount of baking powder to your water.

Why are my microgreens wilting?

Wilting microgreens are usually a sign that the plants are receiving too much heat and not enough water. Move your tray away from the heat source and make sure they are being watered sufficiently.

Why are my microgreens pale and yellow?

Pale and yellow microgreens are a sign that the plants are not receiving enough sunlight or nutrients. If you are relying on natural light and you consistently find your microgreens to be pale and yellow, you may need to switch or supplement with an artificial light source. If the lighting isn't the issue, consider using a soil that contains more nutrients or adding nutrients to the soil. This is more common among microgreens that take longer to reach maturity, such as cilantro and basil that take longer than 2-3 weeks to grow.

Why are my microgreens growing so slowly?

The most common reason for slow microgreen growth is that the temperature is too cold. Try moving your microgreen trays to a warmer location. Something as simple as placing a towel underneath your microgreen tray can be enough to limit heat from escaping. Alternatively, use heated mats.

Why do my microgreens have dry or burned sections?

When you notice dry or burned sections on the leaves of your microgreens, try moving your trays slightly further away from the light source. Burned or dry microgreens are a sign that your plants are either getting light too early in the germination process or are simply too close to the light during the growing phase.

Why are my microgreens bending or falling over?

The most common cause of microgreens bending or falling over is a lack of hydration. Make sure to be attentive to your crop. Pay attention to the color and consistency of your soil, as this will be a good indicator of how well your plants are hydrated before there is a problem.

3) Selling Your Microgreens FAQs

What are the initial start-up expenses of a microgreens business?

You can find more detailed information relating to starting your microgreen business from Chapter 7 onwards, including advice from Don DiLillo of Finest Foods NY & DonnyGreens.com. The good news is that a microgreen business does not involve a sizeable financial outlay since microgreens do not take up a lot of space and don't require expensive or specialized equipment. Most people who choose to start a commercial microgreen farming business can get going for less than $1,000 (in the U.S for example). Keep reading to see what Don, the expert, has to say about the matter.

Which are the easiest microgreens to start with?

Some microgreens are easier to grow than others, which is why many people choose to start with pea, broccoli, or radish. When starting out commercially, it's a good idea to gauge the interest of local buyers and begin growing the varieties that are in demand in your local area. Then, learn to perfect your crops as early as you can.

Is a microgreen business profitable?

Don DiLillo, the founder of Finest Foods, generates revenue of more than $8,000 per month by selling microgreens door-to-door through his local delivery service. Now, he has employees to manage the whole operation and no longer needs to focus his full attention on the business. In the U.S., for example, it is not unreasonable to expect to turn a profit of $2,000 per month following a simple home-based microgreen operation, even without any employees. The profitability of a microgreen business relies to a large extent on the "evergreen" nature of the business, with full-time growers able to produce as many as 25 crop cycles each year, thanks to the short growth cycle. As these crops have a high value per pound in comparison to fully grown vegetables, there is a high potential for profitability.

CHAPTER 6

Simple Home Microgreen Recipes

It's time to take advantage of the tremendous health benefits that microgreens offer, as well as the incredible flavor profiles that microgreens boast. In this chapter, you'll be introduced to a vast range of incredibly tasty recipes that you can easily prepare at home. Let's delve in.

SMASHED AVOCADO TOAST

Ingredients

- 2 slices of wholemeal bread
- 1 ripe avocado
- 1 cup of rainbow swiss chard microgreens
- Balsamic glaze
- Salt
- Crushed red pepper

Method

1. Smash the avocado flesh and add salt
2. Toast the bread, spread lavishly with smashed avocado
3. Top with microgreens, sprinkle with red pepper and drizzle over some balsamic glaze

PEA SHOOT PANCAKES

Ingredients

- 3 eggs
- 1 cup of cottage cheese
- 2 tbsp of EVOO (extra virgin olive oil)
- ½ cup of chickpea flour
- 1 minced garlic clove
- 2 tsp of lemon zest
- ½ tsp of salt
- 1 cup of chopped pea shoot microgreens
- 3 tbsp of chopped chive microgreens

Method

1. Blend the eggs, cottage cheese, EVOO, flour, garlic, lemon zest, and salt in a blender

2. Pulse in the pea shoot and chive microgreens

3. Add the blended pancake batter ¼ cup at a time to a greased pan and cook until bubbles begin to form

4. Flip the pancakes and cook for a further minute until both sides are browned

CHICKPEA, BELL PEPPER & CILANTRO FAJITAS

Ingredients

- 3 sliced bell peppers
- 1 sliced yellow onion
- 2 cups of cooked chickpeas
- 3 tbsp of EVOO (extra virgin olive oil)
- 1 tbsp of chili powder
- ½ tsp of garlic powder
- ¼ tsp of cumin
- Salt
- 8 corn tortillas
- Cilantro microgreens
- Hot sauce

Method

1. Preheat your oven to 450°F (232°C), and line a baking tray with baking paper

2. Add the bell peppers, onion, and chickpeas into a bowl

3. Drizzle with EVOO, sprinkle the chili powder, garlic powder, cumin, and salt and stir until evenly coated. Add the contents of the bowl to your baking tray.

4. Roast for 20 minutes, turning once

5. Fill tortillas with bell peppers, onion, and chickpeas, then top with hot sauce and cilantro microgreens

LEMON & GARLIC PASTA WITH ARUGULA & PARSLEY MICROGREENS

Ingredients

- 1 lb. of dry spaghetti
- ½ cup of EVOO (extra virgin olive oil)
- 2 tbsp of butter
- 1 tbsp of minced garlic
- 1 tbsp of grated lemon peel
- ¼ cup of lemon juice
- ¼ cup of chicken broth
- 2 tsp of dried basil
- Salt and pepper
- 1 cup of arugula microgreens
- ½ cup of chopped parsley

Method

1. Heat the spaghetti in a large pot of salted boiling water for 10 minutes
2. Heat EVOO and butter together in a small saucepan
3. Stir in the garlic, lemon peel, lemon juice, broth, basil, salt and pepper and bring to boil
4. Reduce the heat and simmer for 3 minutes
5. Drain the pasta and pour the sauce over the top
6. Add arugula and parsley, toss until combined
7. Serve with salt, pepper, and lemon juice

MOZZARELLA, PESTO & FRESH ARUGULA PIZZA

Ingredients
- 3 cups of all-purpose flour
- ½ tsp of active yeast
- 1 ½ tsp of salt
- 1 ¼ cup of water
- Fresh mozzarella
- 1 large sliced tomato
- Handful of prosciutto
- ½ cup of arugula microgreens

Method
1. Mix the first four ingredients in a large bowl to create the dough, adding more water if the dough is too rough
2. Cover bowl using plastic wrap at room temperature for 12-24 hours, the dough should double in size
3. Form the stretchy, sticky dough into a pizza base
4. Add the main toppings, then bake for 12-15 minutes at 500°F (260°C)
5. Sprinkle on arugula microgreens after removing the pizza from the oven

SPICY RICOTTA & PARMESAN PIZZA WITH PISTACHIO NUTS & BACON

Ingredients

- ½ cup of ricotta cheese
- ½ cup of grated parmesan cheese
- 2 tbsp of EVOO
- ½ tsp of pepper, freshly ground
- ¼ tsp of sea salt
- ¼ cup of pistachios, chopped
- 4 strips of smoked bacon, sliced into 1-2" strips
- ½ cup of southern giant mustard microgreens

Method

1. Preheat the oven to 500°F (260°C)
2. Prepare the dough
3. Combine ricotta, parmesan, olive oil, sea salt & pepper in a bowl
4. Mix well, then spread the mixture across the pizza base
5. Add the bacon and half of the pistachio nuts
6. Bake for 12-15 minutes until the dough is browned and bacon is crispy
7. Garnish with remaining pistachios and southern giant mustard microgreens. These will add an extra kick of spice and flavor.

SALMON & MICROGREEN BURGER

Ingredients
- Brioche buns
- Salmon fillets or salmon patties
- Tzatziki
- Red leaf lettuce
- Tomato slices
- Cucumber slices
- Spring onion and radish microgreens

Method
1. Lightly toast the buns
2. Cook the salmon fillets or patties to taste
3. Layer the bun with the lettuce and tomato, then the salmon, tzatziki, cucumber, radish and spring onion microgreens

GRILLED BRIE & HAM SANDWICH WITH KOHLRABI MICROGREENS

Ingredients

- 2 tbsp of butter
- 2 slices of brioche bread
- 4 slices of ham
- 6 slices of brie
- 6 thin slices of apple
- 1 handful of kohlrabi
- 1 tbsp of mustard

Method

1. Add butter to pan, heat until it melts
2. Add bread to pan, then place the brie and ham slices on top
3. Grill until cheese melts and the bread is golden
4. Add apple, mustard and kohlrabi microgreens on top
5. Place the second slice of bread to complete the sandwich
6. Flip the sandwich and serve when the second slice of bread is golden

SALMON & THYME MICROGREEN PATTIES

Ingredients
- 1 lb. of deboned salmon
- ¼ cup of diced onion
- ¼ cup of finely chopped cilantro or parsley microgreens
- 2 ½ tsp of sumac
- 2 tsp of lemon juice
- 2 tsp of chopped thyme microgreen
- 1 egg
- ¼ cup of breadcrumbs
- Salt and pepper

Method
1. Combine chopped salmon and vegetable ingredients in a large mixing bowl
2. Form into patties
3. Coat each patty in egg and breadcrumbs
4. Lightly fry on each side

BROCCOLI & KIMKRAUT SALAD WITH LIME HUMMUS

Ingredients
- 1 cup of broccoli microgreens
- ½ cup of kimkraut
- ¼ avocado, sliced into small pieces
- 1 tbsp of salted sunflower seeds
- 2 tbsp of homemade vinaigrette
- 2 tbsp of lime hummus (or plain hummus with lime juice)

Method
1. Place microgreens on a plate, top with avocado slices, sunflower seeds and kimkraut
2. Drizzle with vinaigrette, sprinkle with black pepper and place the hummus beside

RAINBOW BEET & BASIL MICROGREEN SALAD

Ingredients

- 8 small rainbow beets
- Canola oil
- 2 cups of basil microgreens
- ¼ cup of olive oil
- Juice from ½ a lemon
- Salt
- 1 tbsp of chopped pistachios
- 1 cup of various microgreens

Method

1. Toss rainbow beets with canola oil
2. Roast beets at 350°F (176°C) for 30-45 minutes until charred
3. Allow it to cool
4. Remove beet skins
5. Slice beets into quarters
6. Combine olive oil, lemon juice, and basil microgreens in a blender to create fresh basil olive oil
7. Arrange beets on a plate, sprinkle with pistachios and drizzle with basil olive oil
8. Garnish with any additional microgreens of your choice!

ARUGULA, CAPER & ASPARAGUS SALAD

Ingredients
- 3 ½ cups of arugula microgreens
- 1 cup of blackberries
- 2 tbsp of pine nuts
- 1 ear of red corn
- ½ cup of white asparagus
- 2 tbsp of EVOO (extra virgin olive oil)
- 1 tbsp of red wine vinegar
- 1 clove of pressed garlic
- 2 tbsp of chopped caper berries
- 1 ½ of tbsp chopped mint
- Salt and pepper

Method

1. Combine the EVOO, red wine vinegar, mint, garlic, caper berries, and salt in a bowl, store in the refrigerator

2. Trim the asparagus ends, lightly coat with EVOO, sprinkle with salt and pepper, then grill

3. Cut into short segments

4. Add the asparagus and salad ingredients into a bowl, then drizzle with salad dressing

WILD RICE & MIXED MICROGREENS SALAD

Ingredients

- ½ cup of wild rice
- ½ cup of brown rice
- ½ cup of spring onion microgreens
- ½ cup of parsley microgreens
- ½ cup of coriander microgreens
- ½ cup of dill microgreens
- 1 chopped red onion
- 2 tbsp of olive oil
- ¼ cup of blanched almonds
- ¼ cup of raisins
- Salt and pepper
- ¼ cup of lemon juice
- ¼ cup of EVOO (extra virgin olive oil)

Method

1. Soak raisins overnight in cold water
2. Cook rice, fluff with a fork, and transfer to a large bowl
3. Fry the red onion in EVOO until golden brown, then transfer to bowl with rice
4. In the same pan toast almonds and raisins, then add to rice bowl
5. Add all remaining salad and microgreens to the bowl of rice, mix thoroughly
6. Season with salt and pepper, then add lemon juice and EVOO

RADISH & BEET MICROGREEN SMOOTHIE

Ingredients

- ¼ cup of beet top microgreens
- ½ cup of pea shoots
- ⅛ tsp of oregano
- ¼ cup of radish microgreens
- 1 banana
- ½ of a cubed mango
- 6 cups of orange juice
- 1 cup of yogurt
- 1 tbsp of honey

Method

1. Process all the ingredients in a blender, serve into a chilled glass over ice

KALE, ALMOND & CHOCOLATE SMOOTHIE

Ingredients
- ¾ cups of chocolate-flavored rice or almond milk
- 1 banana
- 2 tsp of cacao powder
- 1 tbsp of almond butter
- 1 cup of kale microgreens
- ¼ tsp of cinnamon

Method
1. Combine all ingredients in a blender, serve over ice into a chilled glass

BROCCOLI MICROGREEN & POTATO SOUP

Ingredients

- 1 tbsp of EVOO (extra virgin olive oil)
- 1 chopped onion
- 2 diced garlic cloves
- 2 diced celery stalks
- 1 oz. of rum (optional)
- 3 cups of water 2 cups of broccoli and cauliflower microgreens
- 1 tbsp of parsley
- ½ tsp of thyme
- Salt
- 1 cubed potato
- 2 chopped carrots

Method

1. Add the EVOO to a pot and heat
2. And the onions, celery, garlic, rum and water to the pot
3. Cook for 1 hour or until onions are soft
4. Add microgreens and cook for 1 hour
5. Mix in spices and salt
6. Transfer to a blender, blend but do not puree, then return to pot
7. Add carrots and potatoes
8. Cook for 4 hours then serve

SUNFLOWER GUACAMOLE

Ingredients

- 2 avocados
- ½ a lime, juiced
- ¼ tsp of salt
- ⅔ cup of sunflower microgreens
- ¼ cup of red onion microgreens
- ½ of a jalapeno pepper

Method

1. Mash the avocado with lime juice and salt
2. Lightly chop and then stir in sunflower microgreens, red onion microgreens, and jalapenos

MICROGREEN INFUSED PESTO

Ingredients

- ¼ cup of pumpkin seeds
- 2 cups of kale or basil microgreens
- 2 cups of sunflower or sweet pea microgreens
- 2 cloves of minced garlic
- 3 tbsp of lemon juice
- 2 tbsp of balsamic vinaigrette
- ¾ cup of EVOO (extra virgin olive oil)
- ¼ cup of chopped red onion
- ½ cup of ground nuts
- ½ cup of grated Romano cheese

Method

1. Pulse the pumpkin seeds in a blender until finely ground then set aside
2. Process the microgreens, garlic, lemon juice, vinaigrette, salt and ½ cup of EVOO in blender until the greens begin to grind
3. Gradually drizzle any remaining EVOO into the processor
4. Stop and stir with spatula as needed
5. Stop when blended but not pureed, then transfer to large bowl
6. Lightly stir in nuts and Romano cheese
7. Store in the refrigerator for 24 hours to allow flavor to intensify

SUNFLOWER MICROGREEN SALSA

Ingredients
- 1 cup of sunflower microgreens
- 6 cherry tomatoes
- 1 chopped onion
- Chopped cilantro
- 1 tbsp lime juice
- 2 chopped jalapeno peppers
- 7 chopped serrano peppers

Method
1. Combine ingredients in a blender, pulse until mixed/chopped, but not pureed
2. Set aside overnight, drain excess liquid before eating

CHOCOLATE STRAWBERRY TART WITH BASIL & GOAT CHEESE

Ingredients
- 1 cup of almond flour
- ½ tsp of salt
- 1 tbsp of cocoa powder
- 2 tbsp (for crust) and 1 tbsp (for filling) of maple syrup
- ¼ cup of melted coconut oil
- 1.5 oz of goats cheese
- 2 tbsp of Greek yoghurt
- 1 ½ cups of strawberries
- ½ cup basil microgreens

Method
1. Whisk together the almond flour and salt
2. Add in the maple syrup and coconut oil
3. Whisk into a crumbly dough
4. Add dough into one medium or two small pie pans, then press down
5. Pierce dough with a fork, multiple times
6. Refrigerate for 30 minutes
7. Oven bake at 350°F (176°C) for 15 minutes
8. Remove and allow to cool
9. Process the goats' cheese, Greek yogurt, and maple syrup in a blender
10. Spread the filling on cooled tart bases
11. Top with strawberries and basil microgreens

CHAPTER 7

Let's Get To Business

By now, your eyes have been opened to the enormous benefits of eating and growing microgreens. You've checked out some fantastic recipes that you can start creating right away. Now the time has come to look at the business side of the microgreen world and to determine whether it might be a potential venture for you to start growing and selling microgreens in your local area.

If you've just skipped to this chapter of the book, chances are you are already accustomed to growing microgreens at home. You will be pleased to know that growing microgreens for business purposes follows the same basic principles as growing for personal consumption. The growing techniques are the same. The equipment and consumables are similar (although everything will need to be purchased on a grander scale with additional items). Most of the problematic aspects of growing microgreens (such as controlling the temperature and humidity of the microclimate) apply regardless of whether you're growing microgreens for your personal use or whether you're growing multiple trays at a time to sell for commercial purposes.

Microgreens are considered one of the most profitable crops to sell due to the high demand and correspondingly high sales value, especially when compared to the low setup costs, low ongoing costs, and the small amount of space and time investment required. There are five significant advantages of creating a business focused on growing and selling microgreens in your local area.

Despite microgreens being tiny in size, they have proven to be one of the most profitable crops on the market. Microgreens are in high demand, causing restaurants, chefs, marketgoers, and discerning consumers to be willing to pay premium prices for these tiny plants. As a niche product, you may even be the first person in your local area to offer microgreens directly to local restaurants and cafés or at your local farmer's market. When you're in the position of being able to provide a quality new product to your market, you'll find that your customers will be happy to pay a premium for your produce.

Microgreens are incredibly healthy. Not only will you feel proud that you are helping people eat a more colorful, nutrient-rich diet, you will also benefit from the increased demand for these nutrient-rich superfoods. This demand will come from local restaurants keen to cater to health-conscious consumers who opt for locally grown and fresh produce. These are fantastic customers and will pay top prices.

It doesn't take all that much space to grow your microgreens, and an entire business venture can even be started with a few vertically stacked trays on a windowsill or in a small spare room of a house or apartment. Of course, you may want to scale up in the future by leasing a professional, commercial space.

Since microgreens can be and are often grown indoors, this is a year-round opportunity. Unlike other types of agriculture, which are usually dependent on the season, climate, and part of the world in which you live, microgreens can be grown and harvested anywhere in the world by using artificial lights and carefully controlling the temperature. With the exception of mushrooms, microgreens are perhaps one of the only crop types that can be successfully grown year-round and in any part of the world—even in colder, winter climates.

Not only can microgreen crops be grown and harvested year-round, but they also have a swift turnaround time. The majority of microgreen varieties grow from the germination phase to harvest in less than ten days. Contrast this with traditional farming of crops like wheat or corn (which typically take an entire season to grow and harvest). A microgreens business gives you the freedom to experiment and test far more due to the short harvesting cycle. You're also able to choose your microgreens based on demand from your local customers rather than being in a position of having to predict future demand three to six months in advance. This saves a lot of guesswork.

We shall go into greater detail about start-up costs that you'll need to take into account when planning your microgreen growing business in the next chapter. Initially, you just need to understand that this is a relatively inexpensive and easy business model to start. If you're not yet sure whether you are ready to begin selling microgreens commercially, know that you can slowly scale up your production from home use to a few local buyers before deciding to go all in.

Unlike many other business opportunities, especially agricultural ones, there is no need to make a full financial commitment and invest your life savings in this business venture. If, however, you are ready to commit fully, a good-sized operation can be up and running for less than $1,000. You may be wondering just how much space your microgreen crops will require and whether you might have enough room in your home? Is it really possible to grow enough microgreen crops in one room of your house or in your basement to begin a small business? You may also be wondering about the time commitment involved with such an undertaking. Will you have the freedom to work your own hours, or will you be stuck at home tending to your microgreen crops all day and night?

Let's first start by addressing concerns about how much space your plants will take up. When you first begin growing microgreens for your consumption, you don't need any more room than a bench or windowsill to place your trays. As you start producing higher volumes of crops to sell commercially, you will either need to find more space to set your trays, or you can take the vertical approach by using racks to stack your trays on top of each other. This is the most efficient and cost-effective way to use your space. It is possible to have over five trays stacked vertically, taking up the same amount of horizontal space as one tray. By setting up your trays in this way, using racks to stack five trays vertically, a floor area of 60 square feet can produce as much as 200 pounds of microgreens in just a two-week cycle.

Let's now address the time commitment required to run a profitable microgreens business. As with all business ventures, the amount of money you generate (and the profit that you retain) is dependent on the amount of time you can dedicate to it, at least initially before any hiring. The amount of time you can put in is, in turn, dependent on your level of commitment and hunger. For example, if you're looking for a side hustle, you can still create a profitable business with a time commitment of fewer than 15 hours per week (that's an average of just over two hours a day) and earn a decent side income. You may, though, desire a smaller time commitment and you can still run a (less) profitable business by devoting 30 minutes of your time every couple of days to tending your crops, plus some time to service one or two recurring clients.

On the other hand, if you're looking to replace your full-time job and earn a high income, you should expect to devote full-time hours to your business. This includes the time taken to grow, maintain, and cultivate your crops, as well as finding potential customers, offering excellent customer service to existing customers, and spending time exhibiting your products at farmer's markets and other community events. To achieve fantastic feats, you must be willing to make considerable sacrifices—at least in the beginning.

A microgreens business is very easy to scale. Once you have the confidence and ability to obtain new clients and customers; all you need to do is scale up your output to suit their demands. At this point, you may even like to look at bringing in some additional help—one or two part-time employees or another full-time employee—to take care of some of the extra tasks. That's what Don from Finest Foods has achieved, leveraging his time to focus on other things now that all of his systems are set up.

If you have excellent people skills, you could leave the growing and cultivation tasks to one of your employees while you take care of finding new customers and servicing your existing customers. If you are more interested in growing excellent crops but aren't as confident when dealing with potential and existing customers, you could hire a sales and marketing employee to take care of the customer service side of your business. At the same time, you are then able to focus your attention on growing the best crops you possibly can.

As with any business venture, you can expect to profit in proportion to the time and energy you put into the business. Since it's up to you to find new customers, you can always increase your gross income—and ultimately your profit—by proactively looking for new channels through which to sell your microgreens. We'll talk about all the most common channels throughout the remainder of this book. So keep on reading. You're more than halfway through now!

The Hardest Aspect of Starting a Commercial Microgreen Business

At this point, you know a lot about growing microgreens but you still probably have plenty of questions. If asked what you imagine would be the hardest aspect of running a commercial microgreens business, what would you say? When we ask this question of other people, answers invariably include variations of the following:

- Knowing which crops to grow
- Choosing the right growing technique, including knowing whether to grow in soil or hydroponically
- Warding off pests and diseases
- Knowing when to harvest crops

The above are genuine concerns that anyone new to microgreens would have. After all, no matter how much academic knowledge you may have about the world of microgreens, it is only through practice and trial and error that you can perfect your methods and become a real expert. That's why I always encourage people to start growing their first crops as soon as possible, even if you're not yet sure which crops you're going to sell commercially or whether you're ready to commit to a commercial venture at all. It is only once you start growing microgreens that you will truly begin to learn the practical aspects of the business.

Reading this book and having it as a trusty guide will take you a long way, but you MUST apply what you've learned and start taking action to become a successful microgreen farmer. However, the above issues—and others that may be plaguing you with concern right now—are generally not regarded as the hardest aspect of building your microgreen business by industry professionals. If you happened to guess that building relationships with potential buyers and customer service is the hardest aspect, you'd be absolutely correct. It can seem daunting growing microgreen crops from nothing but packets of seeds and bags of potting mix—yet all of that becomes relatively easy with a little time and practice.

Establishing ongoing relationships with business owners and negotiating contracts for standing orders with restaurants and residential customers, however, is a much harder task that can take far longer to perfect.

No matter how good your microgreen crops are, you don't have a business until someone is willing to buy your produce. The whole process begins with market research, which will be discussed in much greater detail in the next chapter. In that chapter, we'll go through the various channels you can sell your microgreens, including restaurants, farmer's markets, grocery stores, and a variety of other channels.

The first step—and arguably the hardest step in establishing your business—will be to carry out your initial market research to find out which potential customers may be keen to purchase your produce on a recurring basis. This will inevitably vary depending on the country you live in and your local area. Some areas will have a higher concentration of high-quality cafés and restaurants, which may open up more opportunities with local chefs and restaurant owners. Other areas may have health-conscious residents and a high preponderance of health food stores. In this case, you may find that health food stores, market shoppers, and residents are your primary clients.

No matter who your clients are, you can make this work. Even if you think you know your catchment area well, you won't know for sure what the overall demand will be for your microgreens until you get yourself out there and start talking to potential buyers. This ultimately involves networking, making contacts, and setting up appointments with local business owners to gauge the level of interest in your product.

While it may seem premature to undertake this step when you haven't yet scaled your microgreen production to a sufficient commercial level, it is a vitally important step to take before ramping up production. After all, there is no point in producing trays and trays of crops for which there is no demand in your local area!

A smart way of approaching local businesses is to bring fresh samples of the microgreen crops you're already producing at home. By doing it this way, the people you're meeting will be able to see that you are a legitimate grower, not just someone testing the waters for a new business idea. Once they've tried your sample, you can then ask them if there are any particular varieties of microgreens that they would be specifically interested in adding to their menus and dishes by purchasing from you.

It's perfectly acceptable to tell a chef or restaurant owner that, while you have plenty of experience growing other types of microgreens, you don't have any existing crops of the particular variety they're looking for. Reassure your potential customer that you will source some good quality seeds and begin cultivating these varieties immediately—stressing that your first batch of crops will take only ten days or less to reach their door.

When you're first starting out with a new microgreen business, it may intuitively seem that you should spend the majority of your time growing crops and perfecting your techniques. While it is certainly important to do this, your primary focus in your early days MUST be on market research and finding potential customers willing to buy your produce. Once you have secured interest or even some initial orders from a few customers, you will be more confident and in a much better position to focus your attention on producing your microgreens.

As an additional note, remember always to keep good records. You'll be making contact with a lot of different cafés and restaurants and speaking with many different people. You might do some door-to-door sales also. I'd recommend that you use an online CRM (Customer Relationship Management) system. In the modern world, this will be the best way to track calls, reminders, and tasks for following up with potential clients. You'll be able to quickly make notes on the go and save important information for later. Arguably, you could use a simple journal or notepad, but that can often be harder to carry around and may be more challenging to stay organized with.

When the time comes to re-establish contact with someone you've already spoken with, you will be grateful for the notes that you took earlier. Taking a few moments to note information will save you the embarrassment of forgetting a business owner's name or confusing one chef's order with another!

Setting Your Prices

You now know that a microgreen business can be a very profitable one, but how much should you charge for your produce? As a general idea, microgreens, on average, will generate a gross income of between $18 and $25 per square foot of crop in the U.S. However, this figure can vary quite considerably depending on the type of crop and the demand in your local area. In this section, we will go into greater detail about setting appropriate and realistic prices for your microgreens.

Your first step when determining a price for your microgreens is to check out the local competition. If there are already businesses/individuals selling microgreens in your local area, find a copy of their price list. If some of your local supermarkets or health food stores are already selling certain varieties of microgreens, take note of their prices. You should set your prices at a similar price to your local market. Too high and you'll price yourself out of the market, too low, and you'll be missing an opportunity to make reasonable profits from your hard work.

If there are no microgreens for sale locally, broaden your search and check the microgreens offered by producers in neighboring towns and cities. Getting a copy of their price list is a good way for you to determine a benchmark rate for your crops. You can always change prices later on. You may choose to keep your crops at a consistent price regardless of the customer, or alternatively, you may like to offer discounted rates in certain circumstances. For example, offering a 10% discount to entice a restaurant, supermarket, or health food store to make a weekly standing order rather than ordering ad-hoc.

When selling at farmer's markets, a simple way of working out whether your pricing is fair, is to note how many people walk away from your stall after hearing your prices. If your products are sensibly priced, you'll find that, on average, one person out of every five will walk away after finding out your prices. In the same way, if five out of five people walk away after learning your prices, your prices are likely much too high. Remember that your ability to keep excellent records is crucial, and this will benefit you greatly as your business continues to grow. In the early stages of production, much of what you do will be trial and error. You'll try different crops and different growing techniques, and you'll experiment with different sales avenues and different pricing structures. By writing down everything you do, you'll have reliable figures to analyze that will assist you in future decision-making for every aspect of your new business.

The easiest way to keep these records is in a spreadsheet. It doesn't need to be fancy, but working with a spreadsheet allows for automated calculations and easy comparisons between different crops and different sales periods. If you prefer to work with pen and paper, keep a notepad and pen with you at all times and write down everything you do. You can always transfer this information to your spreadsheet later. If you're more technologically gifted, input the data directly into your spreadsheet or send yourself an email from your cell phone with new information as it happens.

For each microgreen variety that you grow, record the following:

· The company that you purchased the seeds from, the date of the purchase, the number of seeds you bought, and the price you paid.

· The time and date that you soaked your seeds (if that particular variety requires pre-soaking. See Chapter 12 for a comprehensive list of different seed varieties and which ones need pre-soaking, and for how long).

· The seed density per tray (you can refer to the calculator linked to in Chapter 4 which gives excellent guidance on the correct seed density for many different types of microgreens).

- The growing techniques that you used for that batch, including the type of soil or hydroponic setup, and the stacking position of the tray.
- The environmental conditions at the time throughout the growth phase, including airflow, temperature, and humidity.
- The lighting conditions, including the type of lights you used (natural sunlight or a particular type of artificial light) and the number of hours per day of light the crops received.
- Watering, including how often you watered the crops, the volume of water that you used, and the time of day they were watered.
- The time and date that your crops were harvested, along with the harvesting technique used and your total yield for the tray by weight.

The above information will help you to tweak your growing practices with each batch and determine which unique set of circumstances provide the best yields and, ultimately, the most profit. Similarly, make sure to keep all of your receipts and write down every financial transaction that takes place within your business. Include everything that you paid for initial equipment, ongoing supplies and other expenses. As well as the gross revenue you earn per tray. This information is vital to help you work out your profit margin per tray.

To calculate your profit margin per tray, you first need to know how much it costs you to produce a single tray of microgreens. After you write down the amounts you pay to your suppliers, divide it up into a per tray rate. For example, if you buy a bag of potting mix, keep track of how many trays of microgreens that one bag will service. For example, you may be able to fill 20 trays with one bag of potting mix. You can then divide the cost of that bag among the 20 trays and take this expense into account when working out your net profit. If you later introduce a composting system and start to break down and reuse your soil, you could change your calculations to record how often you need to purchase more soil to replenish your supplies.

Once you begin processing the figures that you have been diligently recording in your spreadsheet, you will come to some very clear (and perhaps surprising) conclusions about which crops are the most profitable for you to sell. It may surprise you to learn that, while you have been focusing on producing several different types of crops to suit your customers' needs, only a few of those crops are bringing in most of your gross revenue. You may even find that some crops are eating into your profits, such as those that require more artificial light or a higher seed density, for example.

CHAPTER 8

Market Research & Planning

Before you can genuinely claim that you run a gardening business selling microgreens, you first need to have a base of customers ready to purchase your microgreen crops. Much of the anxiety that comes with starting a new business can be attributed to the worry that no one will buy what it is you're offering. The sooner you start your market research and begin reaching out to potential customers, the sooner you'll be able to put your plan into action, and the sooner you can start making money. There are several avenues available to sell your microgreens. You may like to start with just one type of customer in the initial stages of your business, or you may want to approach several customer groups to gauge interest levels.

Restaurants

Before approaching restaurants, prepare a flyer with information about your business, the microgreen crops you're producing (or planning to produce), the prices of your products, and detailed information on how they can order from you. Remember that kitchens are busy, messy places, so a small, thin sheet of paper is likely to become wet and discarded. Consider laminating your flyers or even attaching a magnet to the back so they can be displayed on the restaurant's refrigerator door for easy reference. Don't forget to bring them some samples of your microgreens as well. Many restaurants are interested in supporting local producers so that they can advertise this fact on their menus and website. Using locally grown produce is an instant drawcard for a restaurant, so make sure to emphasize that you are based locally and ONLY service local clients.

Never visit a restaurant during their busiest periods. Try to make an appointment to speak with the sous chef during the restaurant's preparation time when it is not yet open to customers. Bring some free samples of your produce so the sous chef can test the quality and flavor of your produce before agreeing to an initial order. Make sure you emphasize that your microgreens will be harvested immediately before delivery so they can be confident they won't receive stored microgreens that may already be a few days old. Once you have secured some initial ad hoc orders from a restaurant, suggest a weekly standing order. This will help you to plan your grows in advance, as well as adding a level of predictable financial stability to your business.

Farmer's Markets

Farmer's markets are another ideal marketplace to sell your microgreens. People attending farmer's markets are looking for fresh, locally grown produce. Microgreen stands also tend to be immensely popular.

You can harvest your crops in the morning before attending the farmer's market or bring your fully grown trays to market so that your customers can watch you harvest and bag up the microgreens in front of them. Since microgreens are a relatively new product, there is a good chance that you could be the first person in your area to sell microgreens at your local farmer's market. Even if other growers follow your lead, there is great benefit in being the first in the area to sell microgreens. If you offer good service and fresh produce, your customers are likely to remain loyal to you even if competitors set up stands nearby.

Grocery Stores

It can be more difficult to get grocery stores to buy your microgreens, but it's certainly an avenue worth pursuing. Independent and smaller grocery stores are more likely to be open to the idea than large chain stores, which is mostly due to more complex regulatory and approval processes found at chain stores.

You could offer to supply the grocery store with a sign advertising locally grown microgreens to be displayed next to your produce. With such a great emphasis on locally grown products, grocery stores may be interested in selling your products as a way of bringing in customers who prefer to shop locally. Similarly, there may be health food stores and fresh juice bars that you can approach regarding a standing order.

Door-to-Door

Door-to-door sales are nowhere near as common today as they used to be but can still be a lucrative way of selling microgreens. The lack of competition may actually be an advantage and homeowners may welcome this approach. Don from Finest Foods NY built up a large proportion of his business through this sales method. He has even found great success in encouraging his customers to eat microgreens on a daily and weekly basis to improve their health.

When you visit, bring free samples with you, along with information about the full range of crops you produce and how people can place orders with you. You should also supply customers with a phone number or email address so they can contact you to place their orders. Additionally, you could set up a simple website with an online ordering system to cater to those who prefer to shop online.

Wholesale

Selling microgreens wholesale is the least profitable method and is best used in conjunction with one or more other sales channels. Wholesalers will buy your microgreens by the tray, saving you the effort of harvesting, washing, and packaging individual orders, but you'll also be earning lower profits in the meantime.

Since you'll be giving over your trays along with the products, make an agreement with the wholesaler about whether your trays will be returned to you at the time of the next order or whether you should add an additional fee to cover the cost of trays. Most wholesalers will have no use for the trays after they've sold the crops, so mentioning this additional cost to cover the trays is an easy way to ensure you will be reimbursed for the trays or the trays will be returned to you.

Costs

No new businesses are immune to start-up costs, which can range from a few basic supplies for under $100 to hundreds of thousands of dollars for pricy equipment or even physical real estate. The good news for those considering starting a microgreen business is that start-up costs are meager, especially when compared to costs incurred when starting most other types of agricultural businesses. Another bonus is that there is no real specialized equipment needed for growing microgreens. The seeds used to grow microgreens are the same seeds that you would use to produce their full-size counterparts and an ordinary high-quality potting mix is perfectly sufficient. In fact, your local hardware store will most likely offer all the products you will need without having to make a unique order. Costs will inevitably vary depending on where you live, but as a general idea, you can expect to incur the following start-up costs:

Growing trays will only cost a few dollars each and can be reused many times over. The number of trays you purchase will depend on the amount of space you have available for growing microgreens and the number of different crop varieties you choose to grow simultaneously.

Seeds are likely to be your most significant ongoing expense, especially as microgreens (being such tiny plants) require a much higher seed density than full-sized vegetable production. While you can purchase most of the seeds you need from your local hardware store, you'll soon find that buying seeds wholesale—whether online or through a special order at a local store—will save you money in the long run. Luckily, seeds are easy to store and don't take up much room, so there is no reason not to purchase a bulk lot of seeds upfront.

For growers relying on **artificial lights**, you'll find that high-quality fluorescent grow lights will cost around $45 each. Again, the number of lights you need to purchase will depend on the number of trays you'll be growing at any time and the amount of space available. If solely relying on natural sunlight, this expense won't apply to you—although it can be beneficial to have some backup artificial lights, as mentioned previously.

Soil will be another ongoing expense. Although you don't need to purchase specialty soil, it is always a good idea to use high-quality soil. If you have sufficient storage room, purchasing soil in bulk can save you money in the long run. If you're only operating from a room of your house, it will be sufficient to replenish your soil as and when. The trays don't require a huge amount of soil, but you will need to change your soil after each crop cycle.

You should also factor in costs associated with setting up a **stand** at a farmer's market if this is one of the sales channels you choose to pursue. Farmer's markets will have a website or a phone number to call to find out about the costs of exhibiting. You will need trestle tables, signs, and a way of exhibiting your products. Also, consider the costs associated with setting up a website and business email address. Additionally, you might want to create and print flyers to give to residential customers, along with order forms, if you choose to use a manual ordering system. In this modern age, this can all be done relatively cheaply.

Finally, you will need to purchase consumable items to package and label your microgreens. Initially, you can start with plastic tubs and blank labels that you can handwrite or run through your home printer. Once you are more established, you may choose to buy these items wholesale to cut costs. Although individual expenses will vary depending on your access to local suppliers, it is safe to estimate that your initial start-up costs for a microgreen business will generally be under US $1,000. Of course, this figure can be greatly reduced by purchasing smaller quantities initially and then using your initial profits to fund subsequent investments.

Choosing Your Crops

With hundreds of different varieties of microgreens available, it can be challenging to know which crops to choose. When starting your growing journey, and before selling commercially, it is recommended that you choose less challenging microgreen varieties such as radish, pea, and broccoli. This will give you a feel for how microgreens grow and an understanding of the process from start to finish. Once you are more experienced and are ready to start growing microgreens commercially, you can conduct some market research to determine the types of microgreen crops that would be most highly sought-after in your local area.

When meeting with sous chefs at local restaurants, tell them which crops you are already producing and ask them which additional varieties of microgreens would be most beneficial to their business. They may already have a dish in mind that could be perfectly complemented by fresh microgreens. Offering to produce the specific crops they need could help you to secure an all-important weekly standing order.

Sourcing Supplies

Some of the equipment and supplies you will need can be sourced from your local hardware store. You will likely be able to find lower prices online if you're willing to wait a little longer for delivery.

There is nothing wrong with starting off buying packets of seeds from your hardware store rather than online. However, you will soon realize that you're spending a lot of money buying multiple packets of seeds to produce only a few trays of microgreens. At this point, you'll realize the value of finding a seed wholesaler. We recommend sourcing several high-quality and affordable bulk seed wholesalers.

The easiest option is to conduct an Internet search by typing 'microgreens seeds' into Google. It can be tempting to create a good relationship with one seed wholesaler and commit to using them for all of your future seed orders. However, remember that the cost of seeds can be the difference between a profitable business and one that is barely breaking even. Rather than remaining loyal to one seed wholesaler (even if they offer a discount or incentive program for large orders), you should get in the habit of comparing prices between various seed wholesalers prior to each order.

An additional benefit of working with more than one wholesaler is that some wholesalers will offer seed varieties that others don't and some may become affected by seed shortages while others won't. Depending on quarantine laws in your country, you may be able to import seeds from overseas. An online search or a phone call to the customs and quarantine department in your country will give you a definitive answer, so you'll know whether you need to look locally or whether you can broaden your search criteria. Whether ordering from overseas or domestically, take into account the average time for orders to be processed and shipped so that you can plan your grows effectively.

A Hobby or a Business?

If you've been growing microgreens for your own consumption for a while, you know how rewarding and enjoyable it can be. Now you're considering scaling your crop production and supplying microgreens to your local area. At this point, there may be a part of you wondering whether you should go ahead with your business idea or whether you should continue growing microgreens for pleasure. After all, it's often the case that a pleasurable activity loses a lot of its enjoyment when the focus shifts from fun to profit. Or perhaps you're entirely new to the world of microgreens and you're wondering whether you should start growing as a hobby first to build up your skills and see if you enjoy the process enough to turn it into a business. Fortunately, a microgreens business is a unique opportunity in that there isn't a tremendous operational difference between growing microgreens for your own consumption and growing enough to sell commercially.

If you're considering starting a microgreen business, some simple advice that has proved useful for many successful microgreen business owners is to keep your business small to begin with. Grow just a few trays of microgreens at a time and test the waters by approaching local restaurants or setting up a stand at a nearby farmer's market. Start with crops that are easy to grow and popular amongst buyers, like sunflowers, radishes, and broccoli. Start too by only buying a couple of artificial lights and raising between five and ten trays per week. Buy your seeds and soil locally rather than ordering wholesale. At this level of production, your commitment is not much greater than it would be if you were growing microgreens for your own use, except for the time taken to contact restaurants and set up a stand at a farmer's market.

The primary point is that there isn't necessarily a world of difference between growing microgreens for your own use and starting to grow them commercially, provided you're happy to start small and expand your production over time. Start with the hard part, which is to conduct your initial market research and contact local restaurants, and then grow your microgreens production to suit your customers' needs and your growing level of interest and orders. In this way, your microgreen production will still feel like a hobby, but you will also be able to test the waters of growing and selling commercially without too much of an initial commitment.

CHAPTER 9

The Great Organic Debate

"Organic" is a word that often gets thrown around in high-end cuisine. People who choose to eat natural food and avoid highly processed meals often look for the word as a sign that the food they're about to eat has been grown and produced with care and is likely to provide nutritional benefits without any harm. "Organic" generally refers to plants that have been produced without using pesticides, fertilizers, or any synthetic chemicals. Just as restaurants and cafés are keen to advertise to their customers that they source locally grown produce, the same holds true for organic food. This then raises the question, *can microgreens be certified as "organic"*?

The great organic debate is contended between soil growers and hydroponic growers. Microgreens growers who choose to grow in soil often argue that soil-grown crops are superior to those grown hydroponically, both in terms of nutritional content and flavor. Soil growers also tend to argue that it is only crops grown in soil that will be eligible for certification as organic produce. Hydroponic growers argue that hydroponic crops have the advantage of being less likely to encounter problems with weeds and pests and have no exposure to soil-borne diseases. However, many hydroponic set-ups use chemical additives and fertilizers in the water. Doing so, therefore, makes crops produced in a hydroponic setup ineligible for certification as organic produce, by definition.

Hydroponic growers must be sure not to use a chemical nutrient solution that isn't OMRI listed in order to have any chance at organic certification. Previously, this was not possible, but with the rapid development of AgTech products, some recent natural nutrient solutions have been made available that *are* allowed to be used for organic farming.

A common misconception about organic food is that it is healthy, nutrient-dense, and basically "good for you." In fact, there is nothing to say that organic food has any nutritional benefits over non-organic food. Why, then, is it considered better to eat foods that have been certified as organic? Organic certification relates more to the recognition that certain herbicides and pesticides haven't been used in the growth and creation of the food. Not only are herbicides and pesticides potentially harmful for human consumption, but their use can harm the environment, particularly when these chemicals make their way into natural water streams.

While it may be possible to have your microgreens certified as organic, the process of certification is likely to be time-consuming, stressful, and expensive. Before embarking down the path of seeking organic certification, ask yourself whether the rewards of being certified as organic will justify the cost, time, and hassle of going through the certification process. Especially since there is no guarantee that your microgreen crops will ever actually qualify for certification. You will also need to weigh up how much more you can charge for your produce once certified organic, compared to the cost of becoming certified.

However, if you choose to buy wholesale organic seeds, you will be assured that your seeds are free from herbicides and pesticides. You can also advertise this fact in your marketing material, which will offer some relief to people who prefer organically farmed vegetables. Although you won't be allowed to use the official USDA organic seal on your packaging in the U.S., for example, a carefully worded statement that your microgreens have been "produced without herbicides and pesticides" and "grown locally from organic seeds" is an honest statement that you have sourced certified organic seeds and then grown those seeds without using herbicides and pesticides.

Of course, care must be taken to ensure that you are not inadvertently causing people to think that your produce is certified as "organic" if you haven't gone through the official process. It is highly recommended that you seek proper legal advice before you add any similar claims to your product's packaging.

CHAPTER 10

Microgreen Economics 101

We've discussed the initial start-up costs for a microgreen business as well as the factors to consider when setting your prices. Now, let's take a closer look at the real economics and potential profits for your microgreen business.

Of course, your costs and potential profits will vary depending on where you live, as well as the level of interest and demand for microgreens in your local area. It will also depend on whether there are other microgreen growers already in business that you will be competing with, along with your ability to source reasonably priced seeds, soil, equipment, and other consumables. You also need to factor in the amount of time you're willing to put into your business, along with any space restrictions you may have. For example, if you only have one small room to grow your microgreens, you'll be limited by the number of trays you can produce each week. Space will have a direct impact on the profitability of your business and your ability to scale over time.

A great place to start this chapter is to talk about pricing. The best method to determine your pricing is to work backward and reverse-engineer. Rather than hazard a guess at what you think might be a reasonable price, it's better to figure out how much money you'd like to make from this business first. Decide how much you'd like to earn per hour of your time, how much per week, per month, and each year, etc. Some people are more ambitious than others. Some growers also have more free time. Some growers have visions of being millionaires, which involves operating multiple farms and employing a large number of staff. Each person's financial goals are different. So first, figure out what you want and figure out how you can get there!

Let's say that you want to earn $25 per hour of your time spent on your microgreen business. For this example, let's assume that you spend around one hour to obtain supplies, plant the seeds, clean up and sell each tray. Remember, this is just a rough guide and you'll get more efficient and faster over time. Your cost per tray is likely to be between $3-5. We'll cover the reasoning for that in the coming paragraphs. Let's use the example of $5 for simplicity. This would mean that you would need to sell each tray for an average price of $30 in order to cover the $5 in costs and to pay yourself $25 for the hour that you worked on each tray. This is not unreasonable, as microgreens typically sell for between $24 to $48 per tray depending on the variety and one tray will likely take much less time to manage than an hour of your time.

Your overhead costs and profit per tray will also vary based on your choice of packaging, seed types and your primary sales method, whether that be door-to-door, a farmer's markets, or direct to fine dining restaurants. For instance, if you're selling at farmer's markets, there's more waste and higher packaging costs due to the fact you are selling in small quantities to a higher number of customers and you might not sell everything you bring. You would also be spending more hours standing at the market and selling. On the other hand, when selling at a farmer's market, you may be able to command higher revenue per tray as you won't be discounting your prices like you would when selling in bulk to restaurants. It's clear that profits per tray can vary wildly depending on these many factors. As you'll learn from Don DiLillo later in Chapter 14, it's best to commit to one sales method and master that first. There's no reason you can't make either one of the options work if you commit to being the best at it. As they say, it's better to be a master of one trade than a jack of many.

Another factor to note in terms of your pricing is *don't be greedy*! If you set your produce prices too high, you'll price yourself out of the market and maybe create a bad reputation for your business. It's best to price a little lower and get your first few customers to generate some sales momentum. If your produce is top quality and your service is unbeatable, your repeat customers won't complain about a small price rise later on.

Now that we have covered pricing principles, let's dive deeper into the numbers to give you a better idea of how much everything costs. Then you'll be a master of microgreen economics and you can enter the market with confidence. A 10" x 20" tray typically costs $5 and represents a fixed cost.

You can likely find cheaper trays but note that they will break easily, resulting in your trays being an ongoing cost rather than an asset for your business. Don recommends investing in high-quality trays from the start.

Aside from the fixed costs that include lighting/fans/timers/pH meters, etc., your three main ongoing expenses will be seeds, soil, and packaging. Most microgreen seeds can be obtained for around $15 per lb., which equates to roughly $1 per tray, assuming a seeding rate of 1oz/tray. High-quality soil (if you choose to grow organically) costs roughly $1 per tray. The cost of packaging varies depending on whether you use plastic boxes, bags, or some other solution. Some of your customers may want to receive their microgreens in recyclable or food-safe packaging, which may bump up your costs slightly. It's also important to understand that other negligible costs would be hard to estimate on a per tray basis, such as water, waste, taxes, and insurance. Therefore spending $1 on seeds, $1 on packaging, $1 on soil (or another growing medium), plus other expenses, means that your costs are going to be in the region of $3-5 per tray.

Considering that you can sell each tray of microgreens for $24 to $48, there's a significant margin for profit in a microgreens business. This is one of the big reasons why operating a microgreens farm can be so lucrative and also explains how Don from Finest Foods can generate over $8,000 per month from just a small urban farm. There aren't many other offline business models or opportunities that offer such large margins.

Furthermore, once your business starts to grow, you'll be

able to hire staff, and it's not unfair to pay them less than you would pay yourself per hour since you are taking on the risk and financial investment as the business owner. As a result, you can pay somebody else to do the labor. This not only frees up your time at an additional cost, but there is still room for profit. Remember, as a business owner, your most valuable asset is your time. Let's illustrate this in numbers.

In the previous example, we used a revenue model of $30 per tray. We subtracted $5 in fixed costs. This left us with $25 per tray to pay ourselves for the time we worked. The difference when staff enter into the equation is that you wouldn't necessarily be paying the staff members as high as $25 an hour. At the time of writing, the minimum wage in the USA is $7.25 per hour. Let's say that you pay your employees more fairly at $13 per hour spent on each tray: $30 subtract $5 in fixed costs equals $25. Then subtract $13 for the employee's labor. You as the business owner are left with $12 profit per tray and you didn't even need to be at the farm growing, watering, or monitoring your microgreens! If you had 100 trays (stacked vertically to conserve space) with one staff member, you would be generating $1,200 in profit per crop cycle. Assuming there are two weeks from germination to making the sale, you could run two crop cycles per month, meaning that you'd be making $2,400 profit every month. Hire more employees and use more growing trays and your monthly profit will only increase!

That brings us to the end of the microgreen economics section. Hopefully, by now, you have a better understanding of the costs, revenue, and profits associated with running a microgreen business. Stay tuned for Chapter 14 where Don will give you his top tips on how he has grown his New York microgreen business from nothing to over $8,000 a month.

CHAPTER 11

Testing, Sterilizing, Storing, Compositing & Labelling

Quality seeds are, without a doubt, one of the most important elements in your microgreen business. Without good quality seeds that will germinate, thrive, and give consistently successful harvests, you won't have any produce to sell. This is why it's so important to source your seeds from a reputable seed producer who can consistently provide high-quality seeds. In Chapter 8, we discussed principles to keep in mind when sourcing your suppliers. In this section, we'll look at seed testing and the specific figures you should look for to determine whether the seeds are worth purchasing.

To legally sell seeds, seed producers are required to include information about the test results for that seed lot on each seed tag. The information on this tag will give you some insight on whether the seeds you're purchasing are worth their asking price. However, the only way to really tell is to test the lot yourself, using your own growing procedures in your own growing environment. To understand the information on a seed tag, there are two important terms you should know: seed viability and seed vigor.

Seed viability refers to the average ability of seeds in that lot to germinate under *ideal* environmental conditions. A warm germination test, also known as the tetrazolium test, is used to test the viability of seeds.

Seed vigor refers to the average ability of seeds in that lot to germinate under stressful conditions. A cold germination test and an accelerated aging test are used to assess the vigor of seeds. This term simply means the amount of "growing power" the seeds have.

Growing microgreens also requires a high seed density, which means that you're going to be using plenty of seeds to produce a single tray of microgreens. The viability and vigor of a particular seed lot is highly valuable information to have as it tells you the average proportion of seeds that are likely to germinate. If these numbers are low, even though you'll be purchasing and using a high number of seeds, only a small proportion of those are likely to germinate and grow successfully. Poor seed quality will also contribute to the chances of mold growth and the loss of trays. Always use high-quality seeds!

Disease Management & Sterilization

Back in Chapter 3, we talked about pest and disease management for both soil-based and hydroponically grown microgreen crops. In this section, let's take a closer look at disease prevention. All microgreens growers will encounter problems with pests, funguses, or molds at one stage or another. Luckily, there are plenty of precautions you can take to reduce your chances of encountering these problems on a regular basis. To understand these precautions, it is first necessary to understand some of the most common sources of disease in a microgreens growing environment. When diseases strike, the cause can almost always be attributed to one or more of the following:

- Above-average humidity
- Unsanitary growing equipment or hands that handle the seeds and crops, or the environment itself
- Imperfect farm procedures
- Seed quality
- Soil/growing medium quality
- Other pathogenic sources

With these sources of disease in mind, the following precautions will help prevent disease in your microgreen growing system:

1) Maintain your farm procedures and farm environment to the highest of standards. These plants are naturally talented at growing—it's what they do. It's up to you, the grower, to ensure that your processes and growing conditions give the plants the best chance of surviving and thriving.

2) Maintaining excellent hygiene in your growing area is an essential step to keeping diseases at bay. This includes keeping your floors clean with daily/weekly mopping, sanitizing your

growing trays between each grow and ensuring that your hands are washed, and food-safe disposable gloves are used each time the microgreen crops or any growing equipment is handled.

If you have been growing microgreens for a while but are suddenly dealing with a new type of disease that you haven't previously encountered, ask yourself what changes may have occurred recently. Did you change an element of your growing routine? Did you start sourcing your seeds from a different supplier? Are you using a different type of potting mix? In Chapter 7, we talked about the importance of keeping meticulous records, both financial and process-specific. By maintaining this habit throughout every aspect of your microgreens business, it will be easy for you to look back at your recent history and identify changes that have occurred prior to a new disease becoming apparent in your crops.

Reusing Equipment

Although most microgreen growing equipment is not overly expensive to purchase, there are clearly some financial benefits associated with reusing equipment as much as possible. Of the different items of equipment needed to grow microgreens, what can you re-use and what should you replace with each new crop cycle? Let's take a closer look.

Growing trays can be reused as many times as desired, provided they are properly washed, dried, and sanitized between each crop. Of course, growing trays will naturally wear down over time due to being handled and subjected to water, light, and heat on a regular basis. You should replace your growing trays in batches to keep costs down, but they can be reused many times before they need to be replaced. Consider investing in stronger, more durable trays that will last a long time instead of cheap trays that break, crack, and warp quickly.

Soil can be reused for multiple batches, providing certain steps are taken. First, remember that when you harvest your microgreens, you are only cutting off the visible upper stem and leaves, leaving the root and seed structure intact. Before you can reuse your soil, it is essential that the remaining seeds and root structures of the previous crop are completely broken down. It is not enough to simply sift the soil to remove the old roots. Any remaining elements of the original crop must be fully composted before the soil can be reused. This can take some time, depending on the specific composting process, but after this, your soil can be reused.

If you are composting the soil yourself, it is important to consider that it is done properly for safety reasons, as well as to kill any unsprouted seeds. Regulations by the U.S. Environmental Protection Agency specify that to achieve a significant reduction of pathogens during composting, the compost should be maintained at minimum operating conditions of 104°F (40°C) for five days, with temperatures exceeding 131°F (55°C) for at least four hours during this five day period.

If using growing pads such as hemp fiber or coconut coir, you'll find that these are generally not reusable. However, they are compostable. If you have a decent composting system, you can add your growing pads to it and reuse them in another form for future crops. Experiments testing the re-use of growing pads have consistently demonstrated low microgreen growth rates. Given the high cost of seeds relative to the cost of growing pads, it makes more sense to compost your growing pads and repurchase new ones for each new crop rather than waste valuable seeds on a reused growing pad.

Microgreen Packaging, Labelling & Storage

Packaging, labeling, and storage are all important topics to study, understand, and master. Let's look at each of these topics in turn.

The way you choose to package your microgreens will have an impact on the legitimacy in which customers view your business, but a lot will also depend on who you are selling your microgreens to, i.e. your target market. Many microgreen growers choose clear resealable plastic bags to deliver their microgreens to their customers, while others choose small plastic containers with lids. While both are viable options, plastic containers with lids are inevitably going to be more expensive to purchase (even on a wholesale basis) than clear resealable plastic bags. However, if you are selling your products at a premium and are looking for the most professional-looking way to present your crops, you may choose to incur the added expense and use containers with lids.

As a general rule, the more information you include on your packaging labels, the better. At a minimum, your packaging should include: the common name or names of the microgreen varieties contained within, any allergens applicable to the microgreens, the net weight, the full list of ingredients (if applicable), the date the microgreens were harvested, and the approximate shelf life of the product. And finally, the full details of your business, including your business name, registered business address, phone number, and website.

It is vitally important that your microgreen products are properly labeled at every stage of the process, from seed germination to crop growing, harvesting and storage, and transportation to your customers. Remember that some people have allergies to certain vegetables, which is likely to mean that they are also allergic to the microgreen version of that same vegetable. Allergies and intolerances aside, your customers will not be too impressed if they've ordered microgreens of one variety and you deliver a different variety to them simply because your crops have not been labeled properly or consistently tracked throughout the growing process.

We discussed storage in greater detail in Chapter 4. For now, let's reiterate that most microgreens stay fresh and edible for about seven days following harvest, provided that they are kept cool and out of direct sunlight. The perfect storage location for microgreens is in your refrigerator. You may need to turn down the temperature inside your refrigerator (if you are able to do so) as microgreens are best kept in a cool environment at about 36°F (2°C).

Safety & Allergies

For the majority of people and under most circumstances, microgreens are perfectly safe to eat. However, there are risks associated with almost every activity in life (even crossing the road) and eating microgreens can harbor some risks that are important to recognize and acknowledge. Knowledge is power, so let's go through some important safety and allergy information concerning microgreen consumption.

The dense growing conditions that microgreens demand can lead to excess moisture and reduced airflow, resulting in an environment more vulnerable to mold and bacterial growth. By now, you know the importance of washing your hands properly before working in the grow room, as well as ensuring that every aspect of your growing environment is kept clean and sanitized through proper farm procedures.

These precautions, along with making sure your seeds are high quality, will be your best defense against E. coli and other pathogens. Sprouts originally got a bad reputation because the seeds being used were contaminated in the first place. Nowadays, all seeds specifically rated for sprouts/microgreens have been triple-tested for pathogens, so make sure your seed supplier is following the same precautions.

Microgreens are miniature, juvenile versions of full-sized plants and vegetables. This unique combination creates an almost contradictory position when it comes to allergies and gluten intolerance. On the one hand, if you're allergic to a particular vegetable, you are most likely allergic to the microgreen version of that same vegetable as well. However, if you have gluten intolerance and would ordinarily avoid gluten-containing plants like wheat and barley, you can usually consume the microgreen version of those plants. This is because gluten is present only in seeds of plants, not the plants themselves. As discussed earlier, you are consuming only the plant when eating microgreens, not the roots or seeds.

With this being said, it is always a good idea to speak

to your doctor or nutritionist before consuming any microgreens if you're concerned about issues regarding allergies or gluten intolerance. If you start to experience symptoms of an allergic reaction following the consumption of microgreens, stop eating them immediately and consult with your doctor.

We mentioned earlier that microgreens can contain as much as 40 times the quantity of nutrients, vitamins, and minerals relative to their full-sized plant and vegetable counterpart. While this is great news for everyday consumers, some people with particular medical conditions or who are taking certain medications need to be vigilant with the quantity of certain vitamins and minerals they consume. For example, vitamin K affects the body's ability to form blood clots. This isn't a concern for most people. Still, people who are taking blood-thinning medications will need to speak to their doctor about safe levels of vitamin K consumption so as not to interfere with the effects of the medication.

Pregnant women are advised to avoid eating certain types of food during their pregnancy, including deli meats, rice (unless freshly cooked), salads (unless washed and prepared), and other types of food that may have a bacterial presence. The greatest bacterial concern for pregnant women is Listeria, a type of bacteria that typically causes no problems in healthy people but can prove harmful or even fatal to pregnant women and their unborn babies. The same concerns affect people with compromised immunity, including people with certain illnesses or medical conditions, the elderly, and young children. If you have any concerns, it's always better to avoid eating raw microgreens. Speak to your doctor to get a better understanding of whether microgreens are safe for you to consume during pregnancy or if you have compromised immunity.

CHAPTER 12

Creating The Perfect Harvesting Conditions

The comprehensive table* below details the optimal conditions and harvest time for many of the most popular and commercially viable microgreens, including whether the seeds need to be pre-soaked prior to planting. There are almost 100 microgreens in this table, giving you ample choice for what you might like to grow and possibly sell as part of your new business venture!

*With credits to: www.microveggy.com/types-of-microgreens

Name	Pre-soak	Flavor	Days to Germinate and harvest

Adzuki Bean	Yes	Rich, sweet, nutty taste	2-3 and 7-8
Alfalfa	No	Mild, nutty, crunchy, pea taste	1-2 and 8-11
Amaranth Red Garnet	No	Beet, earthy taste	2-3 and 8-10
Anise	No	Mild licorice	1-2 and 7-8
Arugula	No	Nutty, peppery	2-3 and 7-10
Asparagus	Yes	Bright, clean, earthy undertones	7-10 and 20-24
Barley	Yes	Mild, earthy, slightly grassy	1-2 and 7-9
Lemon Basil	No	Intense, slightly sweet, spicy, pungent aroma, zesty	2-3 and 10-13
Yellow Beet	Yes	Earthy, similar to beetroot but slightly sweeter	2-3 and 8-12
Borage	No	Cucumber, slightly bitter	4-6 and 10-15

Broccoli	No	Mild, crunchy, dense, slightly bitter	1-2 and 7-10
Long Island Brussel Sprout	No	Mild Brussel sprout flavor, bitter	2-3 and 7-10
Buckwheat	Yes (overnight in cold water)	Tangy, lettuce taste, slightly sour	2-3 and 7-9
Red Pak Choi	Yes	Mild, earthy, slightly sweet, juicy	1-3 and 8-10
Carrot	No	Mild, earthy, vegetable taste	2-3 and 8-14
Cauliflower	No	Mild, peppery	2-3 and 8-12
Celery	Yes (12-24 hrs)	Mild celery taste, sharp, distinctive flavor	5-7 and 13-16
Celosia	No	Mild, earthy	2-3 and 8-12
Bright Lights Rainbow Chard	Yes (8-12 hrs)	Sweet, earthy	1-2 and 8-10

Chervil	No	Mild, subtle parsley/liquorice flavor	2-4 and 16-22
Chia	No	Tangy, slightly bitter, minty	1-2 and 10-12
Chickpea	Yes	Sweet, nut taste	2-3 and 8-12
Chicory	No	Earthy, bitter aftertaste	3-5 and 16-24
Chinese Toon	Yes (24+ hrs)	Mild onion taste	7-10 and 16-24
Chinese Chives	No	Mild garlic taste, slightly sweet/spicy	6-9 and 14-24
Cilantro/Coriander	Yes (4-6 hrs)	Celery taste, strong, citrusy	4-6 and 14-8
Red Clover	No	Mild earthy, nutty, crunchy, juicy	1-2 and 7-12
Vates Collard	No	Mild kale taste, robust	1-2 and 7-10
Persian Cress	No	Peppery, tangy	1-2 and 8-12

Cucumber	No	Juicy, mild cucumber taste	1-2 and 7-12
Red Dandelion	No	Slightly bitter, earthy	2-3 and 12-25
Dill	Yes	Mild dill taste, zesty	4-5 and 12-15
Field Pea / Dun Pea	Yes	Slightly sweet, crunchy, robust flavor	2-3 and 10-15
Green Curled Ruffec Endive	No	Slightly bitter	2-3 and 7-12
Fava	Yes (12-24 hours)	Juicy, crunchy, nutty, sweet taste	3-4 and 12-15
Green fennel	No	Mild liquorice taste, sweet	2-3 and 10-14
Fenugreek	No	Subtle bitter taste, mildly spicy, nutty	2-3 and 10-14
Flax	No	Nutty, mildly spicy	2-3 and 8-12
Hemp	Yes (4-6 hrs)	Nutty, mild	1-2 and 7-10

Red Russian Kale	No	Mild, subtle sweet, broccoli taste	2-3 and 6-10
Purple Kohlrabi	No	Mild, sweet	1-3 and 7-10
Red Komatsuna	No	Rich, slightly sweet	2-3 and 10-14
Leek	No	Strong, mild onion taste, lightly sweet	3-4 and 10-12
Lemon Balm	No	Lemony flavor and scent	3-4 and 14 or more
Lemongrass	No	Strong lemony flavor, sweet	2-3 and >14
Lentils	Yes	Mild bitter, pea taste	2-3 and 7-12
Waldmann's Green Lettuce	No	Mild, rich flavor, some slightly sweet	2-3 and 10-16
Lovage	No	Celery taste, mild, slighty bitter	6-14 and 18-24
Mache	No	Mild, nutty	2-3 and 8-12

Magenta spreen	Yes	Mild	4-8 and 16-25
Gem Marigold	No	Citrus/tangerine-taste, lightly spicy	2-4 and 8-14
Marjoram	No	Zesty, strong, slightly bitter and sweet, similar to oregano but milder and sweeter.	2-3 and 10-14
Mint	No	Sweet, pungent, minty flavor	2-3 and 10-14
Millet	Yes (4-8 hrs)	Mild	1-2 and 12+
Mizuna	No	Mild, light peppery, piquant	1-2 and 8-14
Mung Bean	Yes (8-12 hrs)	Mild bean taste, slightly buttery	1-2 and 7-10
Red giant mustard	No	Sweet, mild spicy	3 and 7-10

Nasturtium	Yes (4-8 hours)	Wasabi spice, intense	2-3 and 8-12
Scallion/Onion	No	Strong, slightly sweet, pungent, mild spicy	3-5 and 12-16
Scarlet Ruby Red Orach	Yes (8-12 hours)	Mild spinach taste, earthy	3-5 and 12-16
Common Italian Oregano	No	Pungent, earthy	5-7 and 16-22
Parsley	Yes	Mild parsley taste, refreshing, succulent	5-7 and 18-30
Tendril Pea	Yes	Mild pea flavor, nutty, slight sweet	2-3 and 8-12
Popcorn	Yes	Sweet, fibrous, crunchy	2-3 and 6-8
Pumpkin	Yes (2-4 hrs)	Mildly nutty, bitter, rich	2-4 and 16+
Red Gruner Purslane	No	Mild tang, spinach taste	3-5 and 10-14

Quinoa	Yes (30 min - 1 hr)	Mild, slightly bitter, earthy	1-2 and 7-12
Hong Vit Radish	No	Peppery	1-2 and 8-10
American Purple Top Rutabaga	No	Peppery, mild	2-3 and 8-12
Sage	No	Earthy, strong, bold flavor	7-10 and 18-25
Salad Burnet	No	Cucumber taste, bland	5-7 and 12-18
Saltwort	No	Mild, earthy	7-10 and 14-20
Sea bean	Yes	Mild, salty, briny	3-5 and 14-25
Sesame	No	Mild	2-3 and 7-10
Britton Shiso (Perilla)	Yes	Liquorice-taste, earthy	3-5 and 8-12
Shungiku	No	Earthy, floral flavor	3-5 and 12-18
Sorrel	No	Lemony, tangy	1-2 and 10-12
Spinach	No	Mild spinach taste	3-5 and 10-14

Black Oil Sunflower	Yes (4 hours)	Nutty	1-2 and 8-12
Tarragon	No	Sweet, liquorice taste	3-7 and 10-14
Tatsoi	No	Mild, slightly mustard taste	1-2 and 8-12
Thyme	No	Earthy, herb taste	8-20 and 25-35
Purple Top White Globe Turnip	No	Mildly sweet, kale taste	2-3 and 8-12
Wasabi	Yes	Spicy, peppery, sharp and strong.	3-5 and 14-21
Wheatgrass	No	Mild sweet, bitter	2-3 and 7-12

CHAPTER 13

Microgreen Marketing & Sales

When you run any kind of small business, you will inevitably wear many hats. Indeed, if you are a sole proprietor, you wear all of the hats, as you are solely responsible for growing your microgreens, finding new customers, and everything in between. For this reason, it can be easy to confuse and combine concepts that would otherwise deserve individual consideration. Think of a large multinational corporation. The sales team would be distinct from the marketing team and may even work on separate floors of a multi-story building. Marketing and sales can seem similar on the surface level, but when you look at the underlying rationale behind each activity, it becomes clear why big companies tend to separate the two activities into independent departments.

Marketing is aimed at increasing awareness of your product, generating new leads, and exciting interest in your business. Examples of marketing initiatives include TV, print, and digital advertising, social media marketing, viral and brand marketing, email marketing, and direct mail. Marketing is generally directed at a wide group of people.

Sales is the process of turning a potential lead into a paying customer. Sales is generally a more personal endeavor, with sales activities aimed at a specific person or group of people. Examples of sales activities include calls, meetings, direct sales, interactions with customers at retail events, and networking.

Keeping this distinction in mind will help you to understand and pinpoint the aim behind every sales or marketing activity you undertake. For example, running an ad in your local newspaper is a marketing activity because it aims to let people know about the microgreen products you offer and how they can get more information. On the other hand, arranging and attending a one-on-one interview with the sous chef at a local restaurant is a sales activity. The aim of the meeting is to persuade the sous chef to purchase your microgreens, preferably with a weekly standing order.

Even though you, as a small business owner, will be undertaking both activities, the distinction between sales and marketing is an important relationship to understand. Knowing whether you are engaging in a sales activity or a marketing activity can help to keep your objective in mind and know what you're trying to achieve with each activity. Ask yourself: *How close am I to converting a potential customer to an actual customer?*

No matter how experienced you are with growing microgreens, you may not have a lot of business experience. A microgreen business—no matter how small and how many customers you service—is still a business and must be managed as such. The following tips will help you to perfect the business aspects of your operation so you can concentrate on growing top-quality microgreens and providing excellent customer service.

Under what name are you going to run your business? When choosing a name, the best advice is to keep it simple. Make it very clear from your name what you do so you don't cause unnecessary confusion. For example, a business name like "Greg's Microgreens" tells everyone that your name is Greg and you sell microgreens. This might be preferable to a clever-sounding name like "Fresh Fascinations," which is only going to leave people confused as to what your business does. On the other hand, keep in mind that each microgreen business owner will have different goals, purposes, and aspirations. Be sure not to limit the perception of what your business does because of your business name. If you want to grow more than just microgreens, you might not want to use the word "microgreens" in the name of your business.

If you plan on creating a website and social media pages to complement your business, do a quick Google search to make sure the domain name and social handles for your chosen business are available before going ahead. It's always a good idea to plan and prepare in advance, but don't take too long to launch your business. It can be tempting to wait until you have perfected growing 5 or 10 different microgreen crops before approaching local businesses and setting up your market stall. However, it's much better to start out small and sell your initial microgreens to one or two customers and then use their feedback to improve and perfect your product. Early customer feedback is one of the best resources you'll have to improve your produce and your business in those crucial early stages.

Your microgreen produce also needs to be excellent for your business to work. As highlighted in Chapter 7, the hardest aspect of running a microgreens growing business is likely to be marketing your products, nurturing leads, generating sales, and providing excellent customer service. With this in mind, take every opportunity you can to perfect your marketing and sales techniques, particularly if you don't have a strong background in these areas. The best way to go about this is to practice with every opportunity and ask for feedback. Enlist the help of your friends and family to role-play various scenarios with you. You'll be astounded at what you can learn and how much your techniques will improve with plenty of practice.

Next, unless people know that your business exists, they can't possibly buy from you. Money follows attention. Your business will rely heavily on your local community to succeed, especially in the beginning, so be sure to develop strong relationships within your local area. Attend every community event you can and always keep flyers and business cards on hand, ready to give out. You never know when you might meet someone who may be interested in your products or services. Something as simple as wearing a T-shirt with your business name when attending community events could be enough to help people know about your business and build brand recognition. Remember that your community probably has a strong online presence as well, so become active in local social media groups. Creating a Facebook page for your business, for example, is completely free. You can then interact with members of your community while building awareness for your brand at the same time.

We have already discussed a wealth of information so far in this book, but maybe you're wondering what exactly you should do first; which steps you should take to get going on the right path? There are many steps you could take to get your new microgreen business off the ground. We'll go through some of those potential first steps here, but it almost doesn't matter which step you take next. What is most important is that you do something—anything—to get the ball rolling!

If you haven't started growing microgreens yet, start by growing your first crop right now. Re-read the step-by-step microgreen growing instructions in Chapter 4, then make a simple shopping list of basic supplies using Chapter 2. Head down to your local hardware store and buy just enough packets of seeds and just enough supplies to support your very first crop. If your microgreens crop is already underway and you're ready to move forward with your business idea, start right now to work on your elevator pitch. This is a short, compelling, and to-the-point introduction to your business and the products that you produce. It is so named because it needs to be short enough to deliver in the time it takes to ride in an elevator with someone. Imagine being alone in an elevator with the sous chef of a local high-end restaurant. You have a unique 30-second opportunity to pitch your business, but you have to make it fast, clear, and compelling. What would you say?

If you're worried about approaching chefs and business owners in your local area, recognize that your concerns are perfectly normal. No matter how good your microgreens are, if you don't have anyone to buy them, then you don't have a business. Before approaching important buyers, practice your delivery as many times as possible. Write a script of what you can say and how you will answer potential questions, queries, and concerns. Play devil's advocate and ask yourself, "What's the worst that could happen? Which questions could they ask me that I don't know how to answer?" Pretend you have been asked these scary questions and work out how you will answer them. Ask your family and friends to role-play with you to give you a chance to practice thinking on your feet. The more you practice and prepare, the better performance you will give when you really are meeting with important buyers.

You might like to try approaching out-of-town business owners and chefs first so you can practice your delivery and increase your confidence before meeting with the all-important buyers in your local area. If you're worried about running a market stall, start by setting up a stand in a neighboring town, so you have some experience when you enter your target area.

Most importantly, give yourself credit for starting. Almost everyone comes up with small business ideas from time to time but few take the next step and move forward to bring their idea into reality. No matter what follows, you are already more successful than everyone else who has an idea but doesn't have the courage or confidence to take the next step.

CHAPTER 14

Guest Chapter with Donny Greens

It's finally time to hear from our guest author, Don DiLillo (Donny Greens)—owner and founder of Finest Foods (FinestFoodsNY.com)—a hugely successful microgreens business based out of Long Island, New York. There's a lot we can learn from Don; his company records impressive sales numbers, reaching six figures in only two years since starting. He's now managed to hire his first couple of employees so that he can focus more of his time on other ventures. At the same time, his microgreens business generates a fantastic income on autopilot.

First, Don will talk about his background and story before giving his five biggest tips for new microgreen business owners. Finally, he'll tell you what he predicts for the future of microgreens and provide you with a couple of methods for which you can make contact with him!

My Story

When I was a young boy, I used to walk through my grandfather's garden picking fresh string beans off the vine and popping them like candy. Naturally, I was drawn to them because this was the freshest food I had tasted. It wasn't until years later that I realized these were some of the most impactful moments of my life. I honestly believe this is where it all started.

I didn't grow up around gardens or organic whole foods. It was only those rare moments at my Grandfather's that I got a taste of the good stuff. My interest in agriculture was sparked during my sophomore year of college in a Global History class. While we were learning about sustainable agriculture, my professor mentioned an urban farmer named Will Allen. Will's methods of farming were very intriguing to me, not only because he used a closed-loop, self-sustaining agricultural system, but also because he wanted to create a system that could be implemented anywhere, even on a basketball court. I decided it would be a good idea to work on a farm to get some hands-on experience in agriculture and see if this spark was really a passion. I worked at Thera Farms for two summers growing tomatoes, eggplants, peppers, beets, and even hydroponic lettuce. Teddy, the owner, didn't think I would last a week, but after being around all the plants and helping facilitate the growing process, I was hooked.

I am very grateful to have had such a positive first experience farming that would solidify my passion and give me the confidence to later start my microgreens business called Finest Foods.

The Beginning

I always knew I wanted to be an entrepreneur, and now that I had uncovered this passion for agriculture, I needed to figure out what I was going to grow. I was constantly scanning and searching the Internet, looking for a profitable crop that I could start growing without too much up-front investment or the need for a lot of space. I finally stumbled across a YouTube video of Nate Dodson (MicrogreensFarmer.com), where he was showing people how to start a business growing microgreens. I knew this was my opportunity, so I got started right away. As I started my business, I was also learning a lot about health. I knew that microgreens were part of the "living foods" group, which are among some of the healthiest foods on the planet. As the boom in health consciousness was rapidly progressing, microgreens seemed like the perfect crop to start growing. The online videos recommended selling to chefs, but I quickly learned that I didn't want to work in that market, seeing as I was more passionate about helping people improve their health. It was this realization that led me to change my business model and pioneer my home-delivery subscription service.

Once I had learned how to grow microgreens, I decided to focus on four principal varieties; pea, sunflower, radish, and broccoli. I started out by tabling at various farmer's markets. This provided an opportunity to get the word out about my company in my local community, and I began building a list of potential customers for my weekly subscription service. In no time, I had a decent customer base, including some health-food stores and juice bars. My business was up and running with little monetary investment, and I quickly outgrew my first grow space, a small section of my parent's basement.

Rapid Growth

I was able to move out of the basement and into an old run-down deli in less than a year from the start of my business. At this point, I had three racks for growing and a fourth for germination, with plenty of space to expand. I focused on growing my subscription service and creating efficient procedures for running my new farm. I began hiring my first round of employees while also developing a new product called the sampler box, which cost $20 and qualified my customers for free delivery. It was an excellent option for people because it contained a little of everything—a variety of flavors and a variety of nutrients. As people are new to eating these foods, this was an easy go-to option that took all the thinking out of their purchase. It quickly became the top seller.

By this point, I was growing on ten racks, and the farm was running very smoothly. I was even able to take a trip to Colorado for a few days, which hadn't been possible since moving into my next (and current) farm. It took about another year to grow out of the deli, find, and move into my new grow space. This was an exciting transition because my business was established, and the new space was a massive upgrade from the deli. I now had a large building that had excellent aesthetics and high ceilings. There was room for over 24 racks, and I was able to design it very efficiently. My farm is now located on the main road rather than a side street, which has created more visibility, translating to more awareness and walk-in traffic.

I moved into the new farm in February 2019, and it took the entire year to finish making upgrades and adjust to the space. I had a client base of over 60 weekly customers, which was covering both my business and personal expenses. Though I didn't focus much on sales, new customers signed up throughout the year, and I earned over $100,000 in sales throughout 2019. I was able to stop attending farmer's markets, which meant that all revenue was coming strictly from my subscription service. Now that my microgreens business was established and successful, I wanted to focus more on my big-picture goals and start setting myself up to achieve them in the future. These goals included inventing a new sprouting device, developing software for microgreens farmers, and launching my personal brand, Donny Greens.

Moving Forward

Over the past few years, I have been able to slowly move my side-projects forward. I have invented and filed two patents on a sprouter, which I am very proud of, and with the help of an investor or a crowdfunding campaign, we will soon be entering the manufacturing phase. I have also been working on the software for microgreen farmers with a professional programmer. This software is based on the excel spreadsheet I created to run my business and will be of great value to microgreens farmers across the world when it is ready to be released sometime in 2020.

By the time you are reading this chapter, I will have videos uploaded on my YouTube channel, and my Donny Greens brand will be growing. The goal is to provide as much value to the microgreens community as possible so that we can get more people growing, and therefore eating, these beautiful plants. I realized I could only grow so much food locally at my urban farm. I decided that my main goal as an entrepreneur is to leave the most significant positive impact I can on our planet and on humankind. By creating educational content, powerful software, and new products, my efforts and impact will be multiplied, resulting in more successful microgreens businesses and more people improving their health with living foods.

What About My Microgreens Business?

Finest Foods is still my baby, my first-born business, and I will continue to grow it and give it the attention it deserves. It is highly profitable and is the driving force behind all of my other ambitions. Moving forward, I would like to add more automation to my grow room to provide more consistency, resilience, and profitability. My goal is to get my farm running entirely on its own, so I can have the freedom to leave for periods of time, work on my various projects, and possibly start a second farm in another state.

Some of my priorities are creating two automated systems, automatic watering, and automatic seed soaking. My top priority is an automatic watering system. To me, watering is the biggest source of human error, and without experience, it is easy to overwater or underwater crops accidentally. This skill is gained more through experience rather than education. An automatic watering system would not only eliminate this source of human error but will keep watering perfectly consistent, as well as reduce labor time and improve schedule flexibility. An automatic seed soaking system would eliminate the need for me to be at my farm every evening, which would further enhance the flexibility of my schedule.

My second priority is hiring a farm manager. Having someone who can effectively run the farm without me is of the utmost value. It gives me my primary resource back—my time. Running a business is not easy and is highly demanding, so having someone to run the internal farm operations would allow me to focus on the bigger picture of my aspirations.

My Top 5 Tips For Starting Your Microgreens Business

1. Take Action & Start Small

You can't start a business unless you actually start growing! How can you expect to start a business if you have never even grown microgreens before? All it takes is some seeds, equipment, and the will to grow. The costs of growing are minimal, so why not start? Don't let the pressures of business stop you from taking that first step. Those pressures can actually take the fun out of growing microgreens. I recommend growing microgreens as a hobby first and experiencing the great pleasure that comes from growing your own food at home. Learn how to use your crops in the foods you are eating. This skill alone will be extremely useful for acquiring and retaining clients because you can demonstrate how to use your products. Most people are not used to incorporating these foods into their diet, so if you have these skills you will be ahead of most other microgreens farmers. Learn this before you have to worry about all the business stuff.

All microgreens businesses start somewhere. All of the successful companies that you look up to started with literally one rack and zero customers. Don't let the success of others intimidate you. You can be successful too if you put in the same amount of time and hard work. Just remember, you cannot have a microgreens business if you don't take ACTION. Buy some materials and seeds and start growing!

Maybe you end up loving growing microgreens but decide you just want to grow for yourself and not start a business. Great! You have now drastically improved your quality of life and have an awesome and unique new hobby. Maybe you learn that you don't like growing microgreens. Good thing you started small and tested the waters before diving into a business and wasting money on start-up costs. Maybe you find that you love growing microgreens and are ready to start your business. Now, you are a capable grower, you've learned how to eat them, and now it's time to find your first customers.

All of these scenarios are great because they are what's meant to be for you, but you will never know until you take action and start growing. Years later, you could have a six-figure business and people reaching out to you about being featured in their book. You just never know!

2. Keep it Simple

There are dozens of microgreen varieties to grow, and

although it is fun and rewarding to try growing them all, this can be overwhelming when starting your business. You should choose a few varieties to start with and master them before trying to sell them to your potential customers. This ensures that you know what to expect during their growth process and will be able to grow the crops to fill your customers' orders. I recommend starting with varieties that are popular and easy to grow. See my YouTube video titled "Best Microgreens To Grow First (EASY & HEALTHY)."

I made sure to narrow my crops down to a few key varieties that each served their purpose. Sweet pea is super easy to grow, and kids love them. They provide high yields and taste like sweet peas, which most people are familiar with. Radish is another easy-to-grow variety that has a spicy kick. I use the "China Rose" variety because they have bright pink stems that are appealing to the eye. Broccoli is relatively easy to grow but slightly more prone to overwatering. I use these because they are a super-healthy variety. They contain a cancer-fighting phytochemical called sulforaphane and have the highest nutrient density of all the microgreen varieties at 40x the nutrients of adult broccoli. The final variety I use is sunflower, simply because of their popularity in the health niche. These require more labor when growing and harvesting because of their shells and also pose issues due to the inconsistent nature of seed quality on the market. If you can get away without growing sunflower, I recommend doing that. From the beginning, I also began growing wheatgrass because of its popularity among health-conscious consumers.

Aside from keeping it simple with your microgreen varieties, it is also essential to keep it simple with your business model. Focus on a specific niche and execute. You can always diversify your customer base as time goes on, but having a simple and focused business model in place will allow you to grow without becoming disorganized and overwhelmed. Do what works for you and go from there. This business really is simple, especially in the beginning—you are growing microgreens and then selling them to customers.

3. Dial in & Focus on Efficiency & Systems

You need a system in place to make your business work. It is this system that you will use over and over again, so make sure it is a well-oiled machine. Do you have a system in place for adding a new customer? What about a system for growing each microgreen variety, knowing when to plant them and when they will be ready for harvest? Running your farm and customer management are the big ones. Make sure you have systems in place so that you know exactly what to do without requiring too much thinking to make it all work. Over time, your systems will change and you will be able to make them better and faster. Start somewhere and put your first systems in place because this is the foundation of how your business will run. They don't have to be perfect, and they won't be, especially in the beginning, but having them in the first place is what's important.

As you start growing microgreens, you will be learning at a rapid rate because everything you are doing will be new. As your brain learns and you improve the systems mentioned above, make sure you are always focusing on efficiency. This is defined as the number of inputs (time, $, supplies) divided by the given output (revenue, yield). You want to be using the least amount of your resources and getting the maximum end result. Why do more work when you don't have to? For instance, you might find that if you water your crop multiple times a day with a small amount of water, you get a higher yield, as compared to watering them once a day with plenty of water. This may seem like a great discovery, but you just added labor time, which might not be efficient, especially as you scale. This may work for a few trays, but what happens when you are watering over 100 at a time!? Make sure your efforts are worth the outcome. Ask yourself if your methods are working currently and will they work as you scale your business.

4. Grow Slowly

Mistakes are inevitable and are at the foundation of learning. Be sure to make your mistakes at the right pace. Otherwise, it could cost you your reputation and even your business. If you have only been growing for a few weeks, do you think it's reasonable to go after a customer like Whole Foods? No. You should be scaling your businesses at a moderate pace and not trying to cut corners or go after deals you don't yet deserve. Because chances are, if you do so, you will make a mistake somewhere, which could cost you in the long term.

Example: There was a person in my town who created a cookie business. She started by approaching a local health food store and they agreed to carry her products. At this point, she did not have a stable recipe in place and wasn't aware of her legal responsibilities. The night before her deadline, she was still trying to perfect the recipe. She was scrambling to get her ingredients and make the perfect batch of cookies.

She managed to meet her deadline but legally didn't have the proper information on her labels. Soon after they made it onto the shelves, the health department visited the health food store and noticed the incorrect labeling and removed the cookies. This reflected negatively on the health food store, which then created a bad relationship with the cookie business. Needless to say, this business tried to expand too quickly, ruining a potential relationship with another business and creating a bad reputation from the start.

Make small mistakes instead of big ones like the mistake mentioned above. You have plenty of time to grow your business; do it right, and don't be greedy. If you want to work with more prominent clients, that's great; set that as a goal and earn your way there. The best way to grow fast is to grow slow and build a strong brand that is respected and trusted. Don't blow your future opportunities by going after them too early.

5. Learn From the Best

I've learned a tremendous amount of information over the past few years about farming, microgreens, business, marketing, accounting, people skills, and plenty more. It is through my experiences that I was able to learn all of this information, and it is my pleasure and honor to share it with you. I'm definitely not the best microgreens farmer, but I have created a successful business by creating my own way of doing things and implementing my own unique business model that fits my passion and situation. I advise you to do the same. Business is a very creative process. You should design your business around your own passions and circumstances. No two companies are the same, and by combining your own set of skills with education from the right teachers, you will have a successful microgreens business in no time.

When I started my business three years ago, there wasn't much information or support. Luckily, there is a ton of content out there to learn from as you start your business. Just make sure to learn from the right educators. Some questions to ask yourself are: how long have they been in business? Are they successful? Is their business model similar to the one you want to create?

You will have to use your best judgment when seeking out information online, but I do have two resources for you. The first is me. I am dedicated to helping grow and support the microgreens community, so if you like my story and like my content, follow me on social and don't hesitate to reach out directly. The second resource is the course found at MicrogreensFarmer.com by Nate Dodson. This is how I got started, and it gave me the necessary tools and information to get started. Nate is a good person and has done a great job cultivating a community around the microgreens business. His course is helpful, thorough, and includes numerous resources that you will be able to use for your business.

The Future of Microgreens

Even though I've already been in business for three years, the microgreens opportunity is JUST BEGINNING. People will always be looking to improve their health. Chefs will always be looking to enhance their dishes. Farmer's markets are not going away any time soon. Veganism and plant-based foods remain on a swift rise. The health revolution is here!

Just like I did, other microgreens farmers will come up with new ways to grow and new business models to pursue. The time is now, and it is only the beginning. *So, what are you waiting for? Get growing!*

Stay In Touch!

To stay informed on the progress of these various projects, follow me on social @DonnyGreens and be sure to subscribe to my mailing list at DonnyGreens.com. You can also join my "Microgreens Support Group" on Facebook to receive guidance, helpful information, and meet other like-minded growers.

Conclusion

Congratulations! You've made it all the way to the end of this book. Not many people will have the dedication that you have shown to get here, so pat yourself on the back. Take a moment to think back to the knowledge you had before you first started reading this book and you'll realize just how much you've learned along the way. Your eyes will have been opened to the exciting world of microgreens. You now understand the significant nutritional benefits of adding microgreens to your diet and how microgreens are an easy and fun way to encourage your children to eat more vegetables and consumable a colorful range of food.

If you were baffled by the idea of creating a profitable microgreens business before you started reading this book, you now understand just how simple the process can be. There are no special seeds to buy, no insanely expensive equipment, and you don't need a lot of space or to live in a specific climate to successfully grow microgreen crops year-round.

In this book, we have covered every aspect of microgreens. We started by looking at what microgreens are (and what they aren't) and mentioned the unprecedented demand for microgreens in restaurants, cafés, and homes across the world. We took a look at the nutritional benefits of eating microgreens before diving into the different techniques used to grow microgreens and the different equipment you need depending on the growing method you choose. That led us to a step-by-step look at how to grow microgreens, from choosing seeds through to harvesting your fully-grown crops. We then tackled some of the most common questions that newcomers have about eating, growing, and selling microgreens before detailing 20 simple and tasty recipes that you can use them in at home.

In the second half of the book, we discussed growing microgreens commercially. From initial considerations such as whether a microgreen growing business is the right choice for you, to whether microgreens will grow in your part of the world, whether you have enough time and space to support a business venture, to the planning and market research stage. We discussed how to choose your crops, how to source suppliers, and how to find the supplies and equipment you'll need to grow your produce. We then took a close look at the financial aspect of the microgreen growing business, covering topics including initial start-up costs, determining where and to whom you will sell your microgreens and some general principles around marketing and sales. Finally, in Chapter 14, we handed the reins over to Don, who detailed how he has been able to build a profitable microgreens business from the ground up. In turn, he's created a business that runs almost on autopilot and makes upwards of $100,000 per year, with plans to grow it even further.

At the outset of this book, we made some pretty big promises. First, we promised that this book would be a one-stop shop and everything you needed to know about every aspect of microgreens. We promised that, after reading this book, you wouldn't need to take any courses, find any additional material, or read any other books about microgreens. It's true, you don't need to buy any courses or read any other books, there's so much information jammed into this book, but self-education and continued development are also vitally important. So we promise we won't get angry if you do decide to read other books or take a look at any online courses such as the one recommended by Don in Chapter 14. We also promised that, once you've finished reading this book, you would have as much knowledge as any expert in the niche area of growing microgreens. Now all you need to do is put that knowledge into practice. There is no reason why you can't start by choosing some easy-to-grow seeds, setting up one or two growing trays, and following the step-by-step instructions outlined in this book. It is only through ample practice and lots of trial and error that you will take your newfound academic knowledge of microgreens and apply it in the real world.

If you only take away one vital piece of knowledge from this book, I hope it's this: microgreens are a delicious powerhouse of nutrients, and they're ridiculously easy to grow, so easy in fact, that anyone in the world, no matter what climate, can create the perfect indoor growing environment to cultivate these truly special and unique family of vegetables.

If you have enjoyed reading this book and enjoyed learning everything there is to know about all aspects of microgreens, please consider leaving a positive five-star review on Amazon. It will mean a lot to us to see that you have enjoyed reading this book as much as we enjoyed writing it. Your positive review will also help get the word out about the nutritional and health benefits of microgreens and potentially inspire other people to incorporate microgreens into their diet and maybe even start a microgreens business of their own (hopefully not in your town, though)!

Thank you, and best wishes on your microgreens journey.

Clive Woods & Donny Greens

References

6 Essential Microgreen Growing Supplies. (2013, June 29). Retrieved January 11, 2020, from https://www.growthis.com/6-essential-microgreen-supplies/

Aaron Marquis. (2019, October 31). The Best Lightings for Microgreens. Retrieved February 6, 2020, from https://www.microveggy.com/light/

Ackley, M. (2016, March 13). Pizza with Pesto, Mozzarella, and Arugula Microgreens. Retrieved February 5, 2020, from https://www.littlewildthingsfarm.com/recipes/2016/3/13/pizza-wi

Alberta Government. (in press). Commercial Microgreens: Production and Best Practices. Agri-Facts. Retrieved from https://www1.agric.gov.ab.ca/$department/deptdocs.nsf/all/agdex15965/$file/268_18-1.pdf

Avocado and Tomato Salad with Microgreens. (2019, December 18). Retrieved January 11, 2020, from https://saladmenu.com/avocado-and-tomato-salad-with-microgreens/

Bredlau, J. (2018, October 3). Microgreen and Kale Zesty Pesto. Retrieved January 11, 2020, from https://www.mysweetgreensmn.com/recipe/microgreen-pesto/

Brenda S. (2015, December 23). Pricing Micro Greens. Retrieved January 11, 2020, from https://backyardriches.com/pricing-micro-greens/

Brighten Your Day With These Delectable Green Smoothies. (2016, January 9). Retrieved January 11, 2020, from http://www.urbancultivator.net/brighten-day-delectable-microgreen-smoothies/

Charred rainbow beet + pistachio salad. (2020, January 11).

Retrieved January 11, 2020, from http://sundaymorningbananapancakes.yummly.com/2013/07/charred-rainbow-beet-pistachio-salad.html

Common Microgreen Diseases and Solutions to Them (FSFS189). (2019, November 15). Retrieved January 11, 2020, from https://paperpot.co/common-microgreen-diseases/

Desmet, H. (2010, February 8). Parmesan and Ricotta Cheese Pizza with Pistachios Bacon and Micro Greens. Retrieved January 11, 2020, from https://whatwelovemost.wordpress.com/2010/02/08/parmesan-and-ricotta-cheese-pizza-with-pistachios-bacon-and-micro-greens/

Diachkova, V. (2018, October 14). Green Vitality Wild Rice Salad. Retrieved January 11, 2020, from https://www.sincerelyv.com/recipes/2018/10/14/x4xy3ikmfumd5droc55jbe1gxdmjpv

Diego, B. (2014, November 4). Making $2000 A Week Growing Microgreens with Luke Callahan. Retrieved January 11, 2020, from https://www.permaculturevoices.com/making-2000-a-week-growing-microgreens-with-luke-callahan-pvp087/

Diehl, A. (n.d.). How to Grow Microgreens from Seed | Gardener's Supply. Retrieved January 11, 2020, from https://www.gardeners.com/how-to/grow-microgreens/7987.html

Dr. Weil - Integrative Medicine, Healthy Lifestyles & Happiness. (2016, December 4). Is Organic Food More Nutritious? Retrieved January 11, 2020, from https://www.drweil.com/health-wellness/balanced-living/gardening/growing-vegetables-hydroponic-or-organic/

Farmer, B. (n.d.). How to Grow Microgreens. Retrieved January 11, 2020, from https://www.bootstrapfarmer.com/blogs/microgreens/how-to-grow-microgreens

Farmer Tony. (2013, December 2). Recipe - Sunflower Microgreen Salsa Verde - Healthy, Spicy. Retrieved January 11, 2020, from http://sproutingseedsoflove.com/microgreen-healthy-recipes-food/recipe-sunflower-microgreen-salsa-verde

Fosdick, D. (2019, July 19). Microgreens are an easy crop you can harvest year-round. Retrieved January 11, 2020, from https://www.dailyherald.com/entlife/20190721/microgreens-are-an-easy-crop-you-can-harvest-year-round

Garlic and Lemon Pasta with Arugula Microgreens. (2017, October

24). Retrieved January 11, 2020, from https://floridamicrogreens.com/garlic-and-lemon-pasta-with-arugula-microgreens/

Desmet, H. (2010, February 8). Parmesan and Ricotta Cheese Pizza with Pistachios Bacon and Micro Greens. Retrieved February 5, 2020, from https://whatwelovemost.wordpress.com/2010/02/08/parmesan-and-ricotta-cheese-pizza-with-pistachios-bacon-and-micro-greens/

Gordon, L. (2014, March 11). Seared Duck Breast with Cranberry Jam. Retrieved January 11, 2020, from https://www.thedailymeal.com/recipes/seared-duck-breast-cranberry-jam-recipe

Greenish Thumb. (2015, March 11). Microgreen Smoothie Recipes. Retrieved January 12, 2020, from http://www.greenishthumb.net/2015/03/microgreen-smoothie-recipes.html

Grilled Cheese With Ham And Brie Cheese With Microgreens, Apple And Dijon recipe. (n.d.). Retrieved January 11, 2020, from https://thefeedfeed.com/eatswithmichael/grilled-cheese-with-ham-and-brie-cheese-with-microgreens-apple-and-dijon

GroCycle. (2019). How To Grow Microgreens For Profit [PDF]. Retrieved from https://grocycle.com/wp-content/uploads/2019/07/How-To-Grow-Microgreens-for-Profit-Ebook.pdf

Grow your own salad. (2012, March 3). Retrieved January 11, 2020, from https://kitchenvignettes.blogspot.com/2012/03/microgreen-salad.html

Growing Your Microgreens Business. (n.d.). Retrieved January 6, 2020, from http://sprouting.com/growing_a_microgreen_business.html#a16562

Harrison, J. (2018, February 21). Microgreens - How to Grow Micro-greens Winter & Summer. Retrieved January 10, 2020, from https://www.allotment-garden.org/gardening-information/microgreens-grow-winter-summer/

Harroch, R. (2015, August 11). 50 Inspirational Quotes For Startups And Entrepreneurs. Retrieved January 10, 2020, from https://www.forbes.com/sites/allbusiness/2014/02/10/50-inspirational-quotes-for-startups-and-entrepreneurs/

Harroch, R. (2017, March 2). 17 Key Lessons For Entrepreneurs Starting A Business. Retrieved January 12,

2020, from https://www.forbes.com/sites/allbusiness/2016/12/16/17-key-lessons-for-entrepreneurs-starting-a-business/

Honeycutt, E. (2017, December 8). Eating The Rainbow: Why A Variety of Fruits and Vegetables Is Important. Retrieved January 11, 2020, from https://foodrevolution.org/blog/eating-the-rainbow-health-benefits/

Johnny's Selected Seeds. (n.d.). Year-Round Microgreens Production for Profit | Johnny's Selected Seeds. Retrieved January 11, 2020, from https://www.johnnyseeds.com/growers-library/vegetables/year-round-micro-greens-production.html

Kadey, M. (2017a, March 3). Pea Shoot Savory Pancakes. Retrieved January 11, 2020, from https://www.alive.com/recipe/pea-shoot-savoury-pancakes/

Kadey, M. (2017b, March 3). Sunflower Guacamole. Retrieved January 11, 2020, from https://www.alive.com/recipe/sunflower-guacamole/

Kelly, K. (2020, January 5). Avocado Toast with Microgreens Recipe. Retrieved January 11, 2020, from https://www.yummly.com/recipe/Avocado-Toast-with-Microgreens-2038283#directions

Kemper, D. (2017, December 14). Smoky Cauliflower Steaks with Tomato Sauce & Microgreens. Retrieved January 11, 2020, from https://www.cleaneatingmag.com/recipes/smoky-cauliflower-steaks-with-tomato-sauce-microgreens

Lake, L. (2019, September 19). The Difference Between Sales and Marketing and How They Work Together. Retrieved January 12, 2020, from https://www.thebalancesmb.com/marketing-vs-sales-what-is-the-difference-2294827

Love, L. (2014, April 22). A Microgreen, Mint + Mango Juice for One. Retrieved January 11, 2020, from http://www.dollyandoatmeal.com/blog/2014/4/21/a-microgreen-mint-mango-juice-for-one

Marketing vs Sales. (n.d.). Retrieved January 12, 2020, from https://www.diffen.com/difference/Marketing_vs_Sales

Marquis, A. (2019a, October 31). Can you reuse the microgreen soil after harvest? Retrieved January 11, 2020, from https://www.microveggy.com/reuse-soil/

Marquis, A. (2019b, October 31). Mold on microgreens? Solved. Retrieved January 11, 2020, from https://www.microveggy.com/mold/

Marquis, A. (2019c, October 31). Selling Microgreens For Profit: Quick

& Easy. Retrieved January 10, 2020, from https://www.microveggy.com/selling-microgreens/

Marquis, A. (2019d, October 31). The Best Lightings for Microgreens. Retrieved January 11, 2020, from https://www.microveggy.com/light/

Marquis, A. (2019e, October 31). The Risk - Are raw microgreens safe to eat? Retrieved January 11, 2020, from https://www.microveggy.com/raw-microgreens/

Marquis, A. (2019, March 1). 100 Microgreens. Retrieved 18 March 2020, from https://www.microveggy.com/types-of-microgreens/

Marquis, A. (2019f, October 31). Where should you grow the microgreens? Retrieved January 11, 2020, from https://www.microveggy.com/where-to-grow/

Marquis, A. (2019g, December 18). Top 100 microgreens: The complete microgreens list for beginners. Retrieved January 12, 2020, from https://www.microveggy.com/types-of-microgreens/

McGrath, C. (2014, March 28). Egg White Omelette with Avocado, Goat Cheese, and Microgreens. Retrieved January 11, 2020, from https://themerrythought.com/recipes/egg-white-omelette-with-avocado-goat-cheese-and-microgreens/

Microgreens Farmer. (2019, July 18). Essential Supplies for Growing Microgreens. Retrieved January 11, 2020, from https://microgreensfarmer.com/essential-supplies-for-growing-microgreen-seeds/

Mini Strawberry Chocolate Tart with Whipped Goat Cheese & Basil Micro Greens. (2016, May 22). Retrieved January 11, 2020, from https://www.vegetarianventures.com/mini-strawberry-chocolate-tart-with-whipped-goat-cheese-basil-micro-greens/

Michael, E. (2018). Grilled Cheese With Ham And Brie Cheese With Microgreens, Apple And Dijon recipe. Retrieved February 5, 2020, from https://thefeedfeed.com/eatswithmichael/grilled-cheese-with-ham-and-brie-cheese-with-microgreens-apple-and-dijon

Moran, N. (2017a, November 29). Managing diseases in microgreens. Retrieved January 5, 2020, from https://www.producegrower.com/article/managing-diseases-in-microgreens/

Mushroom Omelette with Microgreens Recipe. (2020, January 1). Retrieved January 11, 2020, from https://www.yummly.com/recipe/Mushroom-Omelette-with-Microgreens-1192435#directions

Peeling ginger. (2018, March 28). Retrieved January 11, 2020, from https://fooby.ch/en/recipes/15608/pho-bo--beef-and-noodle-soup--with-micro-greens

Poppa John. (2020, January 4). Excellent Vegan Microgreen Soup Recipe. Retrieved January 11, 2020, from https://www.yummly.com/recipe/Excellent-Vegan-Microgreen-Soup-2394968#directions

Pubmeddev. (2016). Interaction of light quality and fertility on biomass, shoot pigmentation and xanthophyll cycle flux in Chinese kale. - PubMed - NCBI. Retrieved February 5, 2020, from https://www.ncbi.nlm.nih.gov/pubmed/27220007

Roasted Broccoli Microgreen Soup. (2017, March 3). Retrieved January 11, 2020, from https://www.alive.com/recipe/roasted-broccoli-microgreen-soup/

Sayner, A. (2019a, June 25). 30 Of The Best Microgreens Recipes Ideas. Retrieved January 10, 2020, from https://grocycle.com/best-microgreens-recipes/

Sayner, A. (2019c, September 10). How To Grow Hydroponic Microgreens Without Soil. Retrieved January 11, 2020, from https://grocycle.com/hydroponic-microgreens/

Sayner, A. (2019d, November 13). Best Growing Medium For Microgreens. Retrieved January 11, 2020, from https://grocycle.com/best-medium-for-microgreens/

Sayner, A. (2019e, November 13). How To Grow Microgreens: The Ultimate Guide. Retrieved January 10, 2020, from https://grocycle.com/how-to-grow-microgreens/

Schneider, L. (2016, July 2). Sumac and Thyme Salmon Burgers. Retrieved January 11, 2020, from http://wildgreensandsardines.com/2014/09/sumac-and-thyme-salmon-burgers.html

Shain, S. (2018, August 27). How You Could Easily Make an Extra $400/Month Selling Tiny Vegetables. Retrieved January 11, 2020, from https://www.thepennyhoarder.com/make-money/side-gigs/microgreens-side-hustle/

Sheet Pan Fajita with Bell Peppers and Chickpeas. (2019, September 30). Retrieved January 11, 2020, from https://withfoodandlove.com/sheet-pan-fajitas/

Shern, R. (2016, July 27). Broccoli Microgreens Salad with Kimkraut,

Avocado, and Lemon Hummus. Retrieved February 5, 2020, from http://minimalwellness.com/microgreens/

Storey, A. (2019, February 14). 6 Ways to Grow Better Microgreens. Retrieved January 11, 2020, from https://university.upstartfarmers.com/blog/6-ways-to-grow-better-microgreens

Stuchiner, G. (n.d.). Rainbow Radish and Edible Flower Salad with Blood Orange Vinaigrette recipe. Retrieved January 11, 2020, from https://thefeedfeed.com/thenonchalantcook/rainbow-radish-and-edible-flower-salad-with-blood-orange-vinaigrette

Verdant Republic. (n.d.). Microgreens FAQ. Retrieved January 8, 2020, from https://www.verdantrepublic.com/microgreens-faq.html

Wallen, C. (2019, January 18). How To Start a Microgreens Business. Retrieved January 11, 2020, from https://www.profitableplantsdigest.com/how-to-start-a-microgreens-business/

Wallin, C. (2019, January 18). Top 10 Questions About Growing Microgreens For Profit. Retrieved January 5, 2020, from https://www.profitableplantsdigest.com/top-10-questions-about-growing-microgreens-for-profit/

What are Microgreens, and Why Should You Care? (2016, March 9). Retrieved January 11, 2020, from http://www.urbancultivator.net/microgreen/

Yates, S. (2013, August 26). End of Summer Salad. Retrieved January 11, 2020, from https://ahouseinthehills.com/2013/8/26/end-of-summer-salad/

Acknowledgements

I would like to acknowledge my wonderful wife Eileen, who has been incredibly encouraging throughout the writing of this book, which has not always been an easy task. And of course, I couldn't leave out my two beautiful girls, Riley and Morgan, who make me so proud every single day.

Clive Woods

Printed in the USA
CPSIA information can be obtained
at www.ICGtesting.com
LVHW092008101023
760721LV00002B/51